Apostle of the Alleghenies

Reverend Demetrius Augustine Gallitzin

by
Margaret and Matthew Bunson

Published by the Diocese of Altoona-Johnstown
126 Logan Blvd.
Hollidaysburg, PA 16648

Copyright © 1999
by the Diocese of Altoona-Johnstown

ALL RIGHTS RESERVED

With the exception of short excerpts for critical reviews, no part of this book may be reproduced or transmitted in any form or by any means, electronic or mechanical, including photocopying, recording, or by any information storage or retrieval system, without permission from the Diocese of Altoona-Johnstown. The authors and the Diocese are grateful to those publishers and and others whose materials, whether in the public domain or protected by copyright laws and utilized throughout, have been included in this work.

Cover design by Robbie Cavolina

Lisa Grote, editor

Acknowledgments

There are many individuals to whom special gratitude is owed for their kind assistance during the preparation of this work. Among them are members of the clergy of the Diocese of Altoona-Johnstown: Msgr. Stanley B. Carson; Msgr. Michael E. Servinsky; Msgr. George B. Flinn; Msgr. Thomas E. Madden, P.A.; Rev. Michael Becker; Rev. Timothy Stein; and Rev. Lubomir Strecok.

Thanks are also owed to: Robert Lockwood, publisher of Our Sunday Visitor; Betty and Frank Seymour for their assistance with research and their friendship and support; Henry O'Brien and Chris Rice of Our Sunday Visitor; Elaine Cicotello, Bishop Adamec's housekeeper (especially for her great hospitality during visits to Altoona); Larry Sutton, Diocesan Director of Finance; Peg Krug of the Prince Gallitzin Chapel House; Marie Cuglietta of the West Charleston Library; Kim Clanton-Green of the Sahara West Library; Msgr. Timothy Dolan, rector of the North American College, Rome; Robbie Cavolina; Jane Cavolina; and Mike Aquilina.

Special gratitude is owed to: Lisa Grote, editor at Our Sunday Visitor, without whose generosity and assistance this book would not have been possible, and Msgr. Paul A. Lenz, Director the Catholic Indian Missions and former pastor of Loretto.

Above all, deep thanks are owed to His Excellency Most Reverend Joseph V. Adamec for his confidence, material and spiritual support, and vision in bringing this project to life.

Table of Contents

Foreword 7
   by Most Reverend Joseph V. Adamec,
   Bishop of Altoona-Johnstown

Introduction 9

Chronology 11

Chapter One
   The Gallitzin Family 15
Chapter Two
   Return to the Fatih 23
Chapter Three
   Into the New World 33
Chapter Four
   The Mission Begins 49
Chapter Five
   To the Clearfields 57
Chapter Six
   Pastor of Loretto 71
Chapter Seven
   Temporal Debts 93
Chapter Eight
   Defense of the Faith 109
Chapter Nine
   The Twilight Era 135
Appendix
   The History of Loretto After Gallitzin 154

Afterword 159

Foreword

It was 1799. The Very Reverend Thomas Heyden of Bedford called the area "the wild, bleak, and inhospitable regions of the Allegheny." But to the Reverend Prince Demetrius A. Gallitzin it had the possibility of a spiritual empire, of a Catholic colony of vast dimensions. It could eminently serve the extension of Christ's Kingdom. And, he would call it Loretto.

For twenty decades, generations have lived with that legacy, a vision that was more than just a dream. Two hundred years later, we of the Diocesan Church of Altoona-Johnstown are the heirs. And not only the heirs but stewards as well. It is into our care that the vision and mission have been entrusted.

One of the noble traits that characterized the Reverend Prince was his ongoing desire to spend all the wealth that was his for the Kingdom of God on evangelization, and on the spreading of God's Word.

Unfortunately, what was his was not his with which to dispose, being cut off from his earthly inheritance. Even this did not dissuade him from placing his very self and all that he did have in service to the Kingdom of God.

As we observe the second centennial of Father Gallitzin's arrival in this portion of the Lord's vineyard, I am indebted to Margaret and Matthew Bunson for their wonderful gift to us. In the *Apostle of the Alleghenies*, they have given us a deeper look into the life of this evangelizer, whose spirit continues to permeate the Church within these mountains. It was for the Church that the Reverend Prince gave up his wealth, his status, and his life.

Most Rev. Joseph V. Adamec
Bishop of Altoona-Johnstown
September 26, 1999

Introduction

The Catholic Church in the United States has been blessed by the presence and labors of many holy priests and religious over the centuries. Prince Demetrius Augustine Gallitzin, the pastor of Loretto, Pennsylvania from 1799 to 1840, stands as one of the most unique of the many individuals called by God to serve the Church in the New World.

We have been honored and edified to have the opportunity to write about the noble apostolate of this priest of God. Fr. Gallitzin was drawn to the mountains of western Pennsylvania not only for their truly inspiring natural and rugged beauty but because of the abiding faith of the people that he found there. He perceived immediately the possibilities for the Catholic Church in the region and chose at the very moment he arrived in the mountains to give himself utterly for the Catholics of the Alleghenies and for the many thousands whom he knew would be drawn to its fertile fields and forests.

Prince Gallitzin devoted forty years of his life to this one place, this one parish. He understood profoundly what the many other Catholic missionaries had themselves long embraced. The Catholic Church in the United States was built one soul, one family, one church, and one parish at a time. Gallitzin worked, struggled, and ultimately prayed unto death for this noble purpose.

His commitment, his solitary labors, and his spirit of prayer challenge every generation of American Catholics. We are grateful to have been a part of the renewed efforts to make this princely pastor known in America.

Margaret and Matthew Bunson

Demetrius Gallitzin, c. 1799

I regret that the Catholics of America do not know the full story of the parish of Loretto, do not know the full greatness of the man. Demetrius Augustine Gallitzin is an honor to the whole priesthood of the Catholic Church.

— Archbishop John Ireland, 1899

Evangelization is a work of the love of Christ, who acts through human beings. America was evangelized by missionaries full of love, whose humility, courage, dedication and holiness, and even the very sacrifice of their lives gave witness to him who is the Way, the Truth and the life.

— Pope John Paul II, 1992

Chronology

1770 December 22, Demetrius Gallitzin is born at the Hague, Netherlands, to Prince Gallitzin, ambassador of Empress Catherine the Great of Russia, and Countess Amalia von Schmettau, daughter of Field Marshal von Schmettau of Prussia.

1780 Demetrius is taken with his sister, Marianne ("Mimi"), to Münster, Germany, for his education.

1787 Demetrius is converted from the Russian Orthodox Church to Roman Catholicism; he subsequently makes his First Communion.

1792 August 18, Demetrius sails to the United States from Rotterdam. November 5, Demetrius enters the Sulpician Seminary in Baltimore under the name Augustine Schmet (Smith).

1795 March 18, Ordination of Demetrius by Bishop John Carroll; Fr. Smith, as he is known, is the first person to receive all orders in the United States. He is posted to the Conewago Mission, in Pennsylvania. While there, he answers a sick call to McGuire's Settlement; he purchases 300 acres from William Holliday.

1799 Bishop Carroll appoints Fr. Smith pastor of McGuire's Settlement. December 25, Fr. Smith says Midnight Mass in the newly constructed St. Michael's Church.

1800 Baptism of the first infant born in McGuire's Settlement, Joseph Bradley, son of Charles and Mary Bradley. Around this time, Fr. Smith established the community of Loretto, in honor of the Shrine of Our Lady in Loreto, Italy.

1802 Fr. Smith becomes a naturalized citizen of the United States.

1803 March 16, death of Prince Gallitzin, Demetrius's father.

1806 April 27, death of Countess Amalia, Demetrius's beloved mother.

1808 Bishop John Carroll is proclaimed by Pope Pius VII the first archbishop of Baltimore.

The diocese of Philadelphia is established, with Michael Egan as its first bishop.

1809 Fr. Smith receives legal permission to resume the use of his real name, Rev. Demetrius Gallitzin.
1811 Bishop Egan visits Loretto and confirms 198 of Fr. Gallitzin's parishioners.
1815 Death of Archbishop John Carroll, archbishop of Baltimore and architect of the Catholic Church in the United States.
1816 Gallitzin publishes his *Defence of Catholic Principles*.
1817 Gallitzin constructs a second, large-frame church at Loretto. Gallitzin's sister, Marianne ("Mimi") marries and so deprives her brother of his rightful inheritance.
1819 Gallitzin publishes *An Appeal to the Protestant Public* in reply to *Vindication of the Doctrines of the Reformation*.
1820 Gallitzin publishes *A Letter to a Protestant Friend on the Holy Scriptures*.
1823 Around this time, Gallitzin is appointed vicar-general of western Pennsylvania.
1824 Death of Gallitzin's sister, Marianne.
1829 Rev. Patrick Rafferty is appointed assistant pastor to Rev. Gallitzin.
1830 Bishop Kenrick is consecrated co-adjutor bishop of Philadelphia. He visits Loretto and leaves a detailed written record of his journeys to the mountain.
1832 Gallitzin oversees construction of a larger house and adjoining chapel, the present Prince Gallitzin Chapel House.
1834 Gallitzin is thrown from his horse and suffers an injury to his leg; the injury is complicated by a hernia from which Gallitzin never recovers. Rev. Peter Lemcke is appointed assistant.
1836 Gallitzin publishes *The Bible: Truth and Charity*.
1840 May 6, Rev. Demetrius Gallitzin dies.
May 9, Burial of Gallitzin.
1843 Creation of the Pittsburgh diocese by Pope Gregory XVI.
1847 Gallitzin's remains are exhumed and moved to a vault outside the church entrance. Franciscan friars arrive at Loretto from Ireland and establish St. Francis School for Boys.
1848 Sisters of Mercy arrive in Loretto.
1853 Sisters of Mercy establish the St. Aloysius School for Girls.
1854 The third church is built at Loretto; it is constructed of brick and dedicated by St. John Neumann, bishop of Philadelphia.

1899 Centennial of the founding of Loretto. Archbishop John Ireland, of St. Paul, Minnesota, dedicates the enlarged and expanded tomb of Rev. Gallitzin. Charles Schwab donates funds and makes possible the construction of the fourth church at Loretto, the present St. Michael's.

1901 Completion of the present St. Michael's Church. The diocese of Altoona is established by Pope Leo XIII; Bishop Eugene Garvey is named its first bishop.

1926 Bishop McCort invites Discalced Carmelite Nuns from France to establish a community in the Altoona diocese.

1930 The Carmelite Monastery of Loretto is completed with funds donated by Charles Schwab.

1940 A pageant is held in honor of Rev. Gallitzin; it follows a Pontifical Mass celebrated by Bishop Guilfoyle.

1951 The Shrine of Our Lady of the Alleghenies is dedicated by Bishop Guilfoyle.

1957 The Diocese of Altoona is renamed the Diocese of Altoona-Johnstown.

1970 Bicentennial of Rev. Gallitzin's birth is celebrated.

1990 The 150th anniversary of the death of Rev. Gallitzin. The Prince Gallitzin Cross Award is established by Bishop Adamec.

1996 St. Michael the Archangel Church is designated a minor basilica by Pope John Paul II.

1999 Bicentennial celebration of the founding of St. Michael's Church by Prince Gallitzin and the birth of Loretto.

2001 100th anniversary of the founding of the Diocese of Altoona-Johnstown.

Chapter One

The Gallitzin Family

After fourteen years in the French royal court of King Louis XVI at Paris and Versailles, Prince Dimitri Alexeievitch Gallitzin, the Envoy Extraordinary of Empress Catherine the Great, departed for St. Petersburg and a triumphant return to the Russian imperial court. The year was 1768, and the forty-year-old ambassador was being given a post of great importance to his tsarina, the empress of all the Russias. He would be named privy councilor of the Enlightenment, a position that mandated him to oversee for all of Russia the adoption of the philosophy and outlook of the dominating movement of the age.

Tsarina Catherine the Great was born in a small principality of Anhalt-Zerbst. She had wed Peter, a German from Holstein-Gottorp, and this union had brought her to Russia when Peter was named heir to Empress Elizabeth. Virtually from the moment he came to the throne in 1762, Peter proved mentally unstable and unwilling to embrace his powers and obligations as tsar. Catherine was horrified by the tsar's behavior and was humiliated by him in public and in private. She understood with great sorrow the devastating influences of Peter's madness, and she knew that his condition would only worsen over time. Catherine brought his reign to a sudden, necessary end when she led the imperial Russian guard in a palace revolt. Peter was deposed and then murdered, and Catherine assumed the imperial throne, ignoring her own young son's claim to the succession.

Once in power, Catherine proved a talented and ruthless empress who saw as one of her tasks advancing the cause of Enlightenment. In this she followed in the footsteps of Emperor Peter the Great I (r. 1682-1725), who had opened his land to the new age by bringing Russia into contact with the West. Peter also founded the city of St. Petersburg as the "Window on the West." In turn, Catherine worked to make the Russian Empire more active and politically powerful in Europe, and enthusiastically promoted the Enlightenment as pronounced by such prominent philosophers as Voltaire, Rousseau, and the encyclopedist Denis Diderot. Enlightenment ideas included greater state control of education and religion and a surge of hostility toward the Roman Catholic Church. In Russia, however, Catherine balanced her policy shrewdly with a deep respect and a wariness for the powerful and influential Orthodox Church.

To organize her programs, she established an actual commission on the Enlightenment, choosing as its head Prince Dimitri. Catherine trusted him completely, as he was one of Russia's most eminent nobles and a devoted adherent of Enlightenment philosophy. However, like Peter the Great, Catherine learned that her policies were too extreme and revolutionary for her subjects and for the conservative Russian Orthodox Church. Western style dominated only at court where French was always the preferred language. Elsewhere in Russia, the common people, especially the serfs, held fast to the old, traditional Russian ways. Thus, Dimitri was faced with an enormous administrative challenge, one that filled him with exhilaration. He was a true aristocrat, raised to such endeavors.

The noble family of Gallitzin traced its distant origins to the Lithuanian Prince Gediminas (r. 1316-1341), who helped to elevate his realm to prominence in northern Europe and established family branches of descendants in Poland, Hungary, and Bohemia, as well as in Russia. The Russian branch gained fame under Prince Andrew Gallitzin (d. 1638), a *boyar* (or noble) serving

The Gallitzin family coat-of-arms.

Courtesy of the Prince Gallitzin Chapel House

Tsar Michael I, one of the first Romanov rulers of Moscow and then all of Russia. While the Romanovs were undisputedly the reigning house of the country, there were few more influential families in Russia than the Gallitzins. While they held prominent posts in the imperial court and in the military, the Gallitzin family remained deeply religious despite this worldly prominence. A member of the family was even the patron saint of Lithuania, St. Casimir (d. 1484), whose remains were enshrined in the Cathedral of Vilnius and who was officially venerated in 1602.

Prince Dimitri Alexeievitch Gallitzin had elected not to follow the customary route of a long military career in Russia, choosing the path of the intellectual achievement and the diplomacy in a new and exciting age. Nevertheless, as a young man he did serve in the traditional post of an officer in the Preobrazhensky Guard, one of the regiments of the Imperial Guard, the troops who protected the tsars. The Preobrazhensky Guardsmen made up the heart of the troops who supported Catherine the Great when she overthrew her husband, Peter. Then the new empress, a widow reportedly through her own doing, paraded before them wearing an insignia of the regiment, and the officer who loaned her his elaborate uniform jacket for the occasion was Dimitri Alexeievitch Gallitzin.

Prince Gallitzin was then given a posting to Turin, Italy, and eventually to Paris, France, as Minister of Extraordinary Affairs. There, in one of the intellectual centers of the age, Gallitzin used his vast wealth to support his favorite writers and philosophers and to acquire art and decorations for the empress, who filled her palace outside St. Petersburg with his gifts. A genuine intellectual, Gallitzin promoted the publication of a treatise on finance and economic matters by Claude Helvetius and even contributed a foreword to it. He became a member of the Imperial Academy of Science in St. Petersburg, enjoying the company of such luminaries as Voltaire, Diderot, Goethe, and Rousseau, and authoring treatises on electricity and mineralogy. His respected work on electricity and his membership in the Freemasons (he was Grand Master of the Oriental Lodge in Paris) brought him into the sphere of the famous American, Benjamin Franklin. This association with the leaders of the Enlightenment did not end with his return to Russia, for once the project in St. Petersburg was completed, Gallitzin was given the highly prized post of Minister Plenipotentiary to Holland, which was then, alongside Paris, a seat of the Enlightenment.

In 1768, Prince Gallitzin returned in triumph from the French court and made a stop at the city of Aix-la-Chapelle, or Aachen, a place known for its healing waters and historical connections to the ancient Holy Roman Empire. The city had the added appeal of playing host for several days to Princess Ferdinand, the sister-in-law of the formidable King of Prussia, Frederick the Great. Several ladies-in-waiting traveled with Princess Ferdinand, including Countess Amalia von Schmettau, who was given deference because of her father, the famed Prussian Field Marshal von Schmettau who had distinguished himself in Frederick the Great's many wars during the previous years.

A portrait of Amalia von Schmettau, by Fr. Becker, 1970.

Prince Gallitzin was captivated almost instantly by the young, beautiful, and intelligent countess. He found her charming, well-mannered, and she demonstrated a spirit of independence that was rather unique for the era. Charming, handsome, and cultured, the prince made up his mind to put aside the customary courtship rituals and to propose to Amalia. This daring act, and his spirit of dominance, won Amalia's heart. She returned his affections and gracefully accepted his offer of marriage. The prince wrote immediately to Berlin to request permission from Amalia's mother and brother, and on Amalia's twentieth birthday, August 28, 1768, they were wed. The couple then set out directly for Russia where they were received by Empress Catherine the Great at St. Petersburg, and Amalia was introduced to the life and culture of Russia.

Amalia von Schmettau was born on August 28, 1748. Her father, the esteemed Field Marshal von Schmettau, the leader of Prussia's armies in the field, was a Lutheran. Her mother, the Baroness von Ruffert was a Catholic. As there were obvious differences in faith, upon their marriage the couple decided that any sons would be raised Lutheran; any daughters would be raised as Catholics. Amalia was thus baptized a Catholic and, after losing her father at a young age, she was sent to a convent boarding school in Breslau, Silesia, where she was known among the nuns for her pious habits and especially for her beauty. The latter was a burden to her for, as she wrote in her diary, one day while walking through the church to make her confession, someone observed that she was "an angel." Even at that tender age, Amalia knew that physical beauty meant very little in the eyes of God and the spiritually wise.

The piety that marked her youth faded gradually as she spent more time in a social environment that discouraged religious zeal in general and Catholicism in particular. Her intelligence and beauty continued to develop, and no less an acute observer than Diderot was able to describe her in her later years as, "very lively . . . very intelligent . . . instructed and full of talents, she has read, she knows several languages, plays on the clavichord, sings like an angel . . . and is exceedingly kind-hearted." Caught up in that spirit of religious indifference which nurtured a devotion not to the true faith but to the Enlightenment, Amalia gave herself to the ideals of the then popular philosophy; however, she remained "an angel" in matters of charity, carefully weighing the truth of events and ideas.

Prince Dimitri Gallitzin introduced Amalia to the glittering Russian court and to his vast estates near Moscow, delighting as well in the opportunity to display to his friends and family the beautiful young woman whom he had won. They were a handsome couple in Moscow, and they were also deemed excellent representatives of the empire. As a result, Prince Gallitzin received another posting — this time to the court of William V, Stadtholder of the Netherlands.

Even before departing from Russia, Amalia received the joyous news that she would give birth to their first child. A daughter, Marianne, was born in Berlin on December 7, 1769, and the family called her "Mimi." The Gallitzins then traveled to the Hague, where they took up residence in Binenhof Palace. After settling into their new posting, Amalia and Dimitri went on to Paris and Switzerland. In March, 1770, they spent time with Voltaire as well. Amalia learned on this occasion that another child was on the way, and, on December 22, 1770, in the Hague, she gave birth to a son.

The child, named Dimitri (or Demetrius), was Prince Dimitri's much desired heir. Nicknamed "Mitri" by the family, he was baptized into the Russian Orthodox Church with the great ceremony and pomp that befitted his rank. Mitri was given the best possible start in life, then a privilege of the aristocracy. Adding luster to his baptismal ceremony was his godmother, Catherine the Great. The foremost diplomats in Europe were in attendance as well, or represented by tokens of their best wishes. Beyond this, there were few ties to his homeland. Once baptized, Mitri was dispatched with his sister to the nursery in the Binenhof Palace, as was the custom. Mitri would never acquire the outlook of the Russian people, centering only on an abiding respect for his family title and position. Indeed, Mitri spoke little Russian, knew virtually nothing about the vast lands of Russia, and had almost no contact with his Russian noble cousins. Like his mother, and, to a great extent, his father, Mitri was a child of Europe rather than of Russia, and like Europe itself, he carried within him the boundless promise of the faith.

His parents went about their activities in fashionably powerful social circles, including state dinners, audiences, lavish balls, and carefully orchestrated receptions. Such an ornate and elegant life had been accepted by the nobles of Europe for centuries, and Prince Dimitri had every reason to expect that he and his wife would

Fr. Gallitzin's birthplace in the Netherlands.

Photo courtesy of Fr. Tim Stein, *The Catholic Register*

carry on this sumptuous lifestyle throughout their marriage. He did not recognize that Amalia was experiencing interior changes prompted by divine grace.

The arrival of her children, combined with the glittering gathering of literati in the Hague, had a curious effect upon Amalia. With each passing gala during the years 1770-1773, she grew more restless and dissatisfied, experiencing an actual envy of the children's governesses, who saw more of Mimi and Mitri than she did. Equally, she regretted the lack of a truly superior education, wishing to improve her mind not only for her own benefit but for the betterment of her children as well.

Such concerns remained hidden until a trusted and respected friend, Denis Diderot, paid a call in 1773. He was on his way to Russia, where Catherine had invited him to take part in her court and to advise on programs of modern education. Diderot adored Amalia, once confiding to a friend: "I love her to madness, and I live in between the prince and his wife as between a kind of brother and a kind of sister." In their heartfelt conversations, Amalia confessed to Diderot that she was increasingly unhappy and longed for a simpler life. Thus, on her behalf, the philosopher took the problem to the prince, something that Amalia would never do. The prince was receptive to her concerns, agreeing that she might adopt a simpler lifestyle to spend more time with Mimi and Mitri, and to devote herself to further education under the direction of any teacher she might choose. Amalia had performed her wifely duties and social obligations with beauty and grace. If she desired a return to pastoral life, such a sentiment was in keeping with the spirit of the time. Dimitri was involved enough in state affairs and had enough responsibilities to keep him occupied. He could afford to be generous and kind.

Amalia's transformation was immediate and dramatic. By the time Diderot returned from Russia, she was different in many ways. Gone were her fine silks, jewels, and elaborate hairstyles. Her life revolved around studies and the education of her children instead. Much of the transformation was her own doing, but part of it was a reflection of the teachings of the Dutch scholar and humanist, Frans Hemsterhuis. He proposed to do away with the empty excesses of aristocratic life and to pursue the study of classical philosophy and the Socratic method in learning. Amalia agreed with him to such an extent that she asked

Diderot to speak yet again to Prince Dimitri. She wanted to leave the palace and to take up residence in a villa outside of the Hague, on the road to Scheveningen, where Dutch nobles owned estates. Here, she proposed, she would maintain some connection with her friends, most importantly her husband and the Princess of Orange, but her primary focus would be her studies and the education of Mimi and Mitri.

Again the prince, who was still preoccupied with his own obligations and used to being alone by this time, consented, and a new home was acquired by the family. Within a short time Amalia was immersed in study and mastered Greek within a matter of weeks. Reassured in her studies, she began to focus her energies on Mimi and Mitri. The next year saw a continuing metamorphosis in Amalia, who believed herself concerned about education and proper disciplines. But in her heart of hearts, Amalia was seeking authority. The Enlightenment ideals and the trappings of rank and power displayed only their shallow origins in the world. Amalia sought the authentic faith and wholeness in the human personality that is bequeathed only by a recognition of the divine presence in human life. Her soul led her on, and in the act of dedicating herself and her children to what was right and true, Amalia set young Mitri on a new course that would lead him halfway around the world to the American frontier.

Chapter Two

Return to the Faith

"I lived during fifteen years in a Catholic country, under a Catholic government.... During a great part of that time I was not a member of the Catholic Church. An intimacy which existed between our family and a celebrated French philosopher, had produced a contempt for religion. Raised in prejudice against Revelation, I felt every disposition to ridicule those very principles and practices which I have adopted since."
                                                                D.A. Gallitzin

The educational methodology that Amalia established for Mimi and especially for Mitri was as extensive and demanding as possible. Strict discipline was enforced in the daily routine, including cold showers. Hemsterhuis gave the children instruction in mathematics and basic astronomy by using the woods and hills to demonstrate the working of the natural world. At night he used the stars in the heavens to instruct his pupils on constellations and cosmic wonders. Amalia, of course, understood that this form of education was temporary because Mitri required more advanced subject matters and a more formal environment.

By 1779, when Mitri approached his tenth year, the age at which formal education normally started, Prince Dimitri and Amalia met to discuss their options. The prince had long before ceased to express his personal opinions about Amalia's daily life, maintaining cordial relations and generously approving of his wife's unusual behavior. However his hopes for Mitri were in keeping with his rank and lineage. He expected his son to be trained in the proper pursuits of a nobleman and to be given a thorough appreciation of his family titles and obligations. When those requirements were established as priorities, the prince was willing to leave the details to his wife.

A cameo of the young Demetrius, age ten.

Committed to everything that would enhance Mitri's education, Amalia initially planned to move to Geneva, Switzerland. This changed when she received a pamphlet on education by Baron Franz von Fürstenberg, Prime Minister of the Princepality of Westphalia, Germany. After corresponding with the Baron, Amalia was invited to the Westphalian city of Münster to examine the schools that had been established there. She was so impressed that by the end of 1779 she had leased a house on Grüne Streiß in Münster from Baron von Fürstenberg. Only a few years before the house had belonged to the Society of Jesus, which had been suppressed in 1774 by Pope Clement

XIV. (That pontiff was under dire threat and intimidation by the crowned heads of Europe who hated the Jesuits for many reasons, above all their devotion to the Holy See.)

Distressed by the bustling activities in the city, Amalia abandoned Grüne Streiß for a leased country estate near Münster at Angelmodde. There she established a school that was considered a genuine model of educational innovation and was much to the delight of Baron von Fürstenberg. Amalia also used her influence and a large number of acquaintances to attract instructors in a host of fields, including mathematics, science, humanities, fencing, riding, and hunting. The success of her endeavor resulted in a long list of families that entrusted their children to her care.

The principal instructor was Amalia, as she took upon herself most of the curriculum. A rising star in some circles of learning, Amalia was noted for her unprepossessing character and her devotion to education. Her fame spread quickly beyond Münster and Westphalia, reaching even the ears of Prince Gallitzin. Despite her public fame, she practiced a personal simplicity, normally dressing as a humble peasant in a shawl and boots. Mimi and Mitri usually wandered the woods without shoes. Once, in fact, a band of peasants, armed with pitchforks, stopped Amalia with her children and briefly threatened her in the erroneous belief that she was a gypsy who had burned down a barn just a short time before.

Mitri remained Amalia's chief concern throughout this period. It was for him and his sister, Mimi, that she had adopted so unusual a lifestyle, and Mitri most certainly enjoyed an upbringing that was unique in his era. Besides having the empress of all the Russias as his godmother, Mitri had the future king of the Netherlands, along with the sons and daughters of powerful nobles and diplomats, as childhood companions in Holland. Thanks to his mother, Mitri also experienced close contact with the other classes and peoples of the era. Mitri played among the sand dunes with the children of farmers, and at Angelmodde he strolled with poor children, sharing both their simple meals of bread and cheese and their adventures of running barefoot in the woods and across the hills. Thus, he knew the realities of life endured by the so-called lower classes, and he had an understanding that human happiness and contentment were not dependent upon station, money, or power.

Amalia also concentrated on Mitri's intellectual and physical development. In keeping with the educational program of von Fürstenberg, Amalia demanded rigid discipline and physical training. Mitri was drilled like a soldier and marched in all kinds of weather, routinely bathing in water that was cold or even icy, much like King Frederick the Great, his distant relative. Again, like the famed monarch, Mitri was trained in riding, fencing, and hunting, as well as in the skills of music and languages.

He mastered several musical instruments including the violin, flute, and clavichord, and learned to speak and read Latin, French, German, and some Italian. If his life was demanding, he knew at each moment that his mother asked nothing of him that she was not willing to endure herself. Amalia shared his drilling and marches, was willing to endure icy waters and rain, and absorbed everything that Mitri was taught. She left virtually nothing to chance, in part because she recognized his great potential, but also out of concern that he fulfill such promise.

Photo courtesy of the Prince Gallitzin Chapel House

The Münster Circle of Princess Amalia. Included in the painting are the princess (center), Marianne Gallitzin (right), and other close advisors to the princess. Fr. Gallitzin is visible in the background, praying before the cross.

A precocious lad, Mitri could be stern of will, much to the confusion of his mother who complained of his being "indolent, and timid, secretive and reserved, entirely without will or energy, creeping about under the influence of others." Demetrius's father echoed this sentiment to some extent, but he took a different perspective, that of the father who was worrying that his son might not follow the path he had appointed for him: "Still waters run deep. I think you mistake his disposition. He is always running against the wind and tide."

Indeed by 1786, the year of Demetrius's sixteenth birthday, both parents were giving serious thought to his future. Prince Gallitzin expected his son to take up a military post, the very one promised to him in the cavalry by Empress Catherine, and then to follow in his footsteps as a diplomat. Amalia had taken steps to placate and satisfy her husband's concerns that Mitri's education had been sufficient in the military arts and in the tools needed for diplomacy. She emphasized the work of Herr Mikel, an expert in fencing and riding in the employ of von Fürstenberg, in training Mitri in the required military skills, and defended her son's abilities in languages.

Two events were to take place that would change Mitri's life dramatically and permanently. The first was the resolve of Amalia to reaffirm once more her own Catholicism, an act that resulted in the conversion of Mitri. The second was the eruption of the French Revolution in 1789, an event that changed the European landscape.

Most converts to the Catholic faith experience joy, elation, and a wonderful feeling of "coming home." Through grace and prayer, such individuals receive the gift of the faith and slowly mature in their spiritual lives. The process for most converts is an internal one essentially, without great social or political upheavals. Relatives might register their dismay or opposition, but such conversions do not become matters of state. For Amalia and Mitri, conversion demanded not only spiritual courage but endurance and a willingness to accept worldly hardships. For Mitri, conversion to the faith was actually the beginning of a unique spiritual journey that would lead him to a new, young land and to the altars of God.

The return of Amalia to the Catholic faith had its origins in her philosophical studies and the examples of charity among her many Catholic friends. Unable to resolve the numerous questions of life and the destiny of the human soul, she found the prevailing philosophy sadly deficient in providing the answers that she sought, while Catholicism offered definite, reasonable, and spiritually motivating solutions. Her years in the convent school, surrounded by piety and prayers, were not entirely forgotten, but Amalia had been led to assume that the Christian religion was incapable of enduring in her time. This outlook began to change gradually as she renewed her acquaintance with Catholic teachings in order to provide well-rounded subjects in her Münster school. Never one to do things half-heartedly, Amalia threw herself into her religious studies and found in the faith the answers she sought.

The von Schmettau family coat-of-arms.

Encouragement and inspiration were provided by friends, Catholics whose charity and sincere concerns impressed Amalia. She also received spiritual guidance from Father Overberg, who answered many spiritual and catechetical questions. Day by day, with deepening prayerful zeal, Amalia was brought back to the faith. Finally, unable to delay for a moment longer, on August 28, 1786, her 38th birthday, she confessed her sins and received Communion with the same enthusiasm as a catechumen receiving her First Communion. She next turned her attention to the spiritual well-being of her children, taking as a model St. Monica, the mother of Augustine (whose feast day was August 28).

Aware of the problems that conversion might cause Mitri with his father and his Russian imperial connections, Amalia nevertheless pressed ahead. She was firmly convinced that the welfare of her children's souls was paramount and far outweighed any concerns for an earthly career. She desired, however, not to merely compel Mitri and Mimi to join her in attending Mass and the other sacraments. She labored with her customary energy to instruct them in the catechism throughout the winter of 1786, and, on Trinity Sunday, she took them to their first confession with the Franciscan priest Father Schnösenberg. They also received Holy Communion. The village priest of Angelmodde wrote of the event:

"I saw a loving Mother kneeling between her two dear ones who were dressed in white clothes. The sight stirred me in such a way that I kept my eyes down to remain in possession of myself. . . . With a full heart, I gave the holy Body of Our Lord to all three and ended thereupon my Mass."

The occasion of the children's First Communion was certainly a day of great joy for Amalia, but the conversion of Mitri was ultimately his own decision and his response to grace. This was made clear in Gallitzin's own words, in an important passage from his "Letter to a Protestant Friend":

> Raised in prejudice against Revelation, I felt every disposition to ridicule those very principles and practices which I have adopted since. I only mention this circumstance to convince you that my observation at that time being of an enemy, not a bigoted member of the Catholic Church, are, in the eyes of a Protestant, the more entitled to credit; and from the same motive, I shall also add, that during those unfortunate years of my infidelity, particular care was taken not to permit any clergyman to come near me . . . I soon felt the necessity of investigating religious systems, in order to find the true one. Although I was born a member of the Greek Orthodox Church, and although all my male relatives were either Greeks or Protestants, yet did I resolve that religion only which, upon impartial inquiry, should appear to me to be the pure religion of Jesus Christ. My choice fell upon the Catholic Church. . . .

Mitri had now begun the long spiritual journey designed for him by Providence. His immediate concern was his father's reaction to the stunning news. The answer came quickly, as Prince Dimitri journeyed to Angelmodde for a family gathering, the first since the conversion. The prince was deeply troubled upon hearing the word of his family's conversion. He worried about the effect that the conversion might have on the position of the Gallitzins in the Russian Empire. Second, there were the inevitable ramifications for his son's own career and life. The prince's own serious distaste of religion added to his consternation about the matter, and he could not but be appalled at the notion of his wife and children abandoning the Enlightenment ideals for Catholicism.

The prince's visit was a time of great stress and emotional strain, but because of his love for his children and wife and his own diplomatic temperament, there were few moments of actual unpleasantness. He addressed his children in what Amalia termed "French compliments," and Amalia felt confident enough in his responses to push him even further. She gave her nightly instruction in the faith with the prince in attendance. This proved too much on several occasions, and the prince interrupted Amalia to assure his children that Christ was to be considered a redeemer only in the way a true philanthropist was a redeemer striving to better the plight of humanity. Amalia's defense of Christ was swift and adamant, and rather than engage in a bitter debate, Prince Dimitri left the house for a stroll in the woods. Later he took a more pragmatic approach and demanded a complete report on Demetrius's education and preparation for military service.

From Prince Dimitri's perspective, military service was a suitable career choice. High rank and preferment were no longer a possibility in the imperial court, for Catholics were most unwelcome and were barred from holding positions in the government. History had already demonstrated the hostility that could be engendered in the Russian court, for earlier in the century Mikhail Alexeievitch Gallitzin had embraced Catholicism while studying in Italy. He had lived quietly once in Russia, but the court heard of his conversion. Tsarina Anna, the stern daughter of Peter the Great, had Mikhail seized, forcibly married to a hideous old woman, and forced to consummate the marriage under bizarre and cruel circumstances.

Mitri had been promised a cavalry position in the Russian army since childhood, but the circumstances of his conversion now rendered such a posting impractical. Nevertheless, the prince was determined to make a soldier of sorts of his son. Mitri certainly demonstrated ability as a fencer and even more so as a rider. He was able to ride with both skill and dexterity, including the difficult maneuver of vaulting over his horse while gripping the saddle. Mitri favored English horses, and an excellent one was secured from von Fürstenberg through the help of a veteran English general named Lloyd when the French Revolution erupted and it appeared possible that Mitri would be called upon to demonstrate his skills.

The Revolution was brought about by severe financial and economic hardships in France, the deteriorating political condition of the monarchy, and the agitation of French society by the currents of revolutionary thinking and writings by such philosophers as Voltaire and Rousseau. What was at first a relatively peaceful movement toward reform in France sank swiftly into upheaval and bloodshed as the radical Jacobin party pushed its way to power, crushed the old order in France, persecuted the Church even to the point of capturing the pope, and finally began executing the nobility, including King Louis XVI and his unpopular wife, Marie Antoinette.

The response of the other European monarchies was predictable; they declared war on France and began a series of campaigns in 1792, ending only in 1815 with the final defeat of Napoleon Bonaparte at the Battle of Waterloo. As the Revolution raged, a flood of refugees from among the French nobility sought safety in the palaces of other European nations. Amalia greeted the early expatriates of France with little compassion because they were mostly wealthy aristocrats who had made the Revolution possible. Once the Revolution grew violent, anti-Catholic, and marked by brutal oppression, she found it impossible to remain inactive. As she witnessed the immense suffering of the simple peasants and humble Catholics fleeing death and persecution, Amalia sold whatever possessions she had available and tried to organize donations from among her acquaintances. An effort to sell Empress Catherine a set of Greek carvings left to her by the late Hemsterhuis was courteously rebuffed.

Mitri, in turn, was aware of the refugees, the horrors of war, and the grave likelihood of his military service now that Europe was aflame with war. His father was disappointed in the bloody and dark turn that the Enlightenment had taken in France, and he was willing to march on the Revolutionaries to restore the old order, even if it meant giving the Church its proper station. Amalia and the prince were thus agreed about the situation in France, and she was even willing to countenance the terrible act of sending Mitri off to war. Her resolve on this led her to have Mitri confirmed in the faith, a desire that she noted in her diary, "which through the near prospect of having to send Mitri to war, took on a new importance."

Prince Gallitzin was subsequently pleased to receive good news from von Fürstenberg that his son would indeed take up military duty — in the Austrian army. Through von Fürstenberg's influence, Mitri was appointed to the staff of the Austrian General von Lillien, then a commander of an army in Brabant, who was preparing for the 1792 campaign against the French. As he prepared himself, Mitri was informed suddenly that the post was closed to him. Emperor Leopold II of Austria had died unexpectedly, and it was suspected that a revolutionary cabal had somehow poisoned him. In 1792, King Gustav III of Sweden had been stabbed to death by a revolutionary named Anherstrom, and in response, the Austrians and Prussians decreed that no foreign soldiers should be permitted to serve in their armies.

Prince Gallitzin still hoped for the cavalry commission that had been promised to his son in the Izmailovsky Regiment of the Imperial Guard. Mitri was expected to set out for St. Petersburg, where he would be accepted at his post, despite his conversion.

While this was agreeable to Prince Dimitri, both Amalia and Mitri heard the news with horror. First and foremost was Mitri's determination not to give his life in the service of a court whose beliefs ran so counter to his own. Moreover, Mitri had never even visited Russia, and his mother's account of life there was hardly conducive to enthusiasm. Last, and of the greatest importance, Mitri was beginning to experience the stirrings of grace, stirrings that called him to the altars of God.

Alert to the dangers of becoming involved in the Russian cavalry, Amalia proposed a solution to the problem. She suggested that Mitri be sent on a "Grand Tour," a custom of the time. Since the traditional tour of Europe was not feasible given the current upheaval and bloodshed, Amalia suggested "Why not send him on a trip to the West Indies and the United States?" Prince Gallitzin once again gave his consent, and it was decided that Mitri should go to America.

Chapter Three

Into the New World

"I never brought to the altar a candidate of Holy Orders about whose vocation I am so certain as I am of your son. This is also the opinion of Bishop Carroll, and of all who know him."
Letter to Amalia from the rector of the Sulpician Seminary, 1792

Having won a reprieve from Mitri's military obligations to Russia, Amalia set about organizing the trip to America with her usual thoroughness. Prince Gallitzin was particularly well-disposed to his son's voyage to the United States, mostly because of the ideas of its leaders: Thomas Jefferson, Benjamin Franklin (his personal acquaintance), and George Washington. Such a trip was in keeping with the training of young nobles and would also aid in the completion of his education, providing him with a wider view of the world and a set of useful experiences for his anticipated future diplomatic labors.

Far more concerned with Mitri's eternal salvation, Amalia saw this journey to the New World as an important step toward manhood and the solidifying of the faith through extended exposure to the cleric that she had chosen to serve as his traveling companion: Reverend Francis Xavier Brosius. This priest had been known to Amalia in his capacity as chaplain and tutor to the noble Droste-Vicherings family. A stolid German, Father Brosius was also a noted mathematician and had an excellent reputation for personal piety and goodness. Father Brosius was on his way to the United States to serve as a missionary, in response to the call issued by the great Bishop John Carroll of Baltimore. The young United States needed German-speaking priests to take the place of the German Jesuits who had left when the Society of

Jesus had been suppressed in 1774. Father Brosius' departure from Europe was imminent, and Amalia hastened to ensure the priest's services as Mitri's guide and traveling companion/tutor.

As always, Amalia was aided by her many friends, all of whom approved of Father Brosius and the proposed trip. Baron von Fürstenberg was especially helpful. Father Brosius had forgotten the name of the ship that was to carry him, and he could not recall the shipping agents. The Baron wrote several letters and soon learned that the name of the vessel was the *Jane,* bound for Baltimore from Rotterdam on the significant date of Amalia's birthday, August 28, 1792. He quickly sent seventy-five guineas to reserve a berth for Mitri and added another five to the seventy already paid by Brosius for his berth, thus assuring a private compartment for the travelers. Von Fürstenberg then wrote to his brother, the Prince-Bishop of Hildesheim-Paderborn, to prepare a letter of introduction to Bishop Carroll on behalf of Mitri.

The only suggestion that von Fürstenberg opposed during all the preparations was that Mitri take another letter of introduction to George Washington from Amalia's brother, who was a general. While von Fürstenberg did not disapprove of Mitri being exposed to the bold, intriguing experiment of democracy in the United States, he was concerned that this impressionable young man might fall victim to excessive hero worship. Not only was Washington the focal point of the American Revolution, he was the first president of the fledgling United States and a formidable figure in the Old and New Worlds.

Mitri grew more and more excited about the impending voyage, although some misgivings surfaced as his departure day approached. Further discussion with his mother led to the decision that he should not travel under his own name. The nobility was believed to be unpopular in America, and Mitri was advised to maintain a certain degree of anonymity. A pseudonym was chosen, taken from his confirmation name and the maiden name of his mother, just three weeks before the ship sailed from Rotterdam. He was to arrive in America as Augustine Schmet (or Schmidt); the name was changed slightly over time to Augustine Smith. In the meantime, the Princess of Orange arrived from the Netherlands with her son, Prince William. Childhood friends, Mitri and William spent days together, and a banquet was organized as the departure neared. Before anyone realized, the day had arrived for Mitri and his mother to begin the slow and emotional trip to Rotterdam.

In later years, Demetrius was fond of describing his last day in Europe. The *Jane* arrived in Rotterdam harbor, and Mitri and Father Brosius made ready to board the vessel as the longboat from the ship was rowed to the dock. At the last moment, Mitri shrank from getting into the boat, overwhelmed with emotion and admitting to his mother, "I do not want to leave." Amalia remonstrated him, crying out, "Mitri! I am ashamed of you." To drive home her disapproval, she pushed him suddenly, catching him completely by surprise. Mitri stumbled backward and could not keep from falling off the dock into the briny water of Rotterdam harbor. An excellent swimmer, Mitri was in no danger of drowning, and he was hauled quickly into the longboat by the laughing sailors.

When Father Brosius was taken on board as well, the longboat rowed back to the *Jane*. Mitri held his gaze on the shore seeking out his distraught but determined mother. As the *Jane* set sail and headed west, Mitri, sopping wet, looked back on the European shore and wondered about the possibilities waiting for him in the distant New World. In later years, Gallitzin called his fall into Rotterdam harbor his "second baptism."

For Amalia, Mitri's sailing was bittersweet. She had struggled for many years to give him the finest possible education and then to instill in him a deep Catholic faith. With her son away, the house at Angelmodde was now painfully empty and her life much less bright. The epitome of her loss was the horse that Mitri had enjoyed riding. The steed was too wild and spirited for Amalia or Mimi, and so went riderless.

She took consolation from two sources beyond that of her abiding religious devotion: the gifts that she had imparted to Mitri and the unexpected visit and the renewal of her friendship with Goethe. The writer and philosopher accompanied Amalia in all of her customary religious activities, demonstrating such care and courtesy that many thought he was himself a Catholic. While his sensitivity to Catholicism was apparent in his writings (in particular his masterpiece *Faust*), he was not moved toward conversion, declaring to Amalia's question on his faith, "I answered mildly and quietly, with my usual credo, so stubbornly opposed to hers. Each of us then took our ways homeward, she with the final wish to see me again somewhere." Angelmodde fell quiet once more, and Amalia's thoughts returned to the sea as Mitri journeyed toward America. She continued to pray for him, unable to know fully the discipline and spiritual grounding that she had given him.

All of her work with her son came to fruition during the weeks that were spent in the cabin of the ship *Jane*. Aboard the *Jane*, in the company of Father Brosius, Mitri was able to see the fullness of the priestly life. Mitri later described his desire for the priesthood, a yearning that arose from the time of his conversion. He had given a hint or two of his vocation to his mother in the months before his departure, but she had dismissed it as a youthful urge and upbraided him for not regarding the priesthood in its true splendor. His father was even more adamant on the subject. Being a convert to Catholicism was unfortunate, the prince admitted, but it was not an insurmountable obstacle to advancement within Orthodox Russia. Should Mitri become a priest, however, the Gallitzin name would be trashed and disgraced and he would be disinherited.

Father Brosius answered Mitri's questions about the priesthood during the long voyage, and the young man was even more devoted when Father Brosius celebrated the Mass. There is little question that by the time the *Jane* crossed the Atlantic, Mitri knew finally and resolutely that he was called to be a priest. Christ had touched his soul with grace, and Mitri had responded. Everything that followed stemmed from that generous surrender.

The *Jane* dropped anchor in Baltimore harbor on October 28, 1792, and the passengers were rowed ashore on the same longboat that had fished Mitri out of the waters of Rotterdam harbor. He and Father Brosius hired a coach and were driven through the unkempt and dismal port town to a small brick structure that bore the nameplate of St. Peter's Church. This was the cathedral church of the recently established diocese of Baltimore. From this *cathedra*, one man headed a diocese that encompassed quite literally the whole of the United States of America, including the vast and dangerous frontier region of the new nation.

Adjacent to the church was a small, humble cottage where the Bishop of Baltimore had his residence. The cottage was in sharp contrast to the lavish baroque palaces occupied by the bishops of Europe,

Old St. Peter's Church, Baltimore, Maryland.

and had the sights and smells of the Baltimore port area and urban avenues not driven home to Mitri the ragged and uncultured state of this new land, the simplicity and plain cottage before him spoke volumes. Mitri quickly discovered that temporal poverty was only an illusory mantle draped upon a profound spiritual and religious vitality.

A knock on the door brought to the portal a white-haired cleric who immediately recognized and welcomed Father Brosius. The bishop spoke to Father Brosius in French and then greeted the young man who stood with him. The youth responded in French and presented several letters of introduction, including the one from the Bishop of Hildesheim-Paderborn and another from Amalia. Mitri was deferential, both because he recognized the position of his host, and because he felt an instant respect for the man who led the new diocese in America: Bishop John Carroll.

John Carroll was a man chosen by God to build the Catholic Church in the young nation, and he came to the task with extraordinary capabilities and a true vision of the faith maturing in the New World. An American, John was born on an estate in Upper Marlborough, Maryland, on January 8, 1735, the third of seven children of Daniel and Eleanor (Darnall) Carroll. Descended from Keane Carroll of Ireland, the family was associated with the dynasty founded by Colonel Henry Darnall, a brother-in-law of Lord Baltimore. The Carrolls were also related to other prominent Catholic families in Maryland and Virginia, and defended the faith vigorously when Protestant bigotry and penal codes threatened.

Charles Carroll of Carrollton, a noted Catholic apologist and a signer of the Declaration of Independence, was a cousin of brothers John and Daniel Carroll. John attended classes at the famed Bohemia Manor with Charles, and in 1748, went on to St. Omer's, in Artois, France, with his cousin. St. Omer's was founded by the Jesuit Robert Persons, a companion of the English martyr St. Edmund Campion, and this venerable institution was an academic haven for exiled Catholic students of England, one of twenty-five such colleges and universities in the world.

Upon graduation, John went to the Watten Jesuit Novitiate, located seven miles from St. Omer's, to begin his religious life of service. He was ordained and professed in the Society of Jesus in February, 1771. Two years later, the Jesuit Order was suppressed by the pope, and John was arrested at Bruges. Lord Arundell, an influential English noble, intervened in the affair, and John was released and allowed to go England to serve as chaplain of the Arundell family in the spring of 1774. Other Jesuits of the period perished or suffered similar disruptions of their priestly lives, the results of the suppression of the order. Strangely enough, Catherine the Great, Mitri's godmother, gave the Jesuits safe haven in Poland (then partly under Russian control) and in White Russia, substantially aiding in the restoration of the Jesuits in 1814 by Pope Pius VII.

In 1774, the future looked grim for the former members of the Society, and John returned to America to live at Rock Creek, the residence of his mother. There were about 22,000 Catholics in the colonies, out of a total population of a recorded 2,205,000. Because Catholics were forbidden public worship, even in Maryland (which had been founded as a Catholic colony), John built a chapel on his mother's property and started discreet missionary work. Cultured, well-educated, and socially-esteemed by the Protestants, he was asked by the Continental Congress to accompany his cousin Charles Carroll, Benjamin Franklin, and Samuel Chase to Canada to ask for aid in the coming efforts in gaining independence. The effort failed miserably as the

Canadians still resented the hostile American reaction to the recent Act of Toleration in matters of religion that had been granted to Canada. Nevertheless, Benjamin Franklin developed a deep respect for John during the trip. He wrote: "As to myself, I find I grow daily more feeble and I think I could hardly have got so far but for Mr. Carroll's friendly assistance and tender care for me."

The Baltimore diocese, the first in the United States, was erected in 1788, and John Carroll was elevated to Bishop of Baltimore by Pope Pius VI, on September 7, 1789. Benjamin Franklin took some credit for the appointment, as he had nominated Carroll for the see in Paris, 1784, during a discussion with the Apostolic Nuncio to France about the state of affairs in the United States. Bishop Carroll started his episcopal labors with courage and determination, anticipating for Catholics "all blessings of justice, peace, plenty, good order and civil and religious liberty."

Archbishop John Carroll, first bishop of the United States and patron of Fr. Gallitzin.

Photo courtesy of Fr. Tim Stein, *The Catholic Register*

This was the prelate who greeted Mitri and Father Brosius in such humble circumstances. Matured by suffering and spiritually attuned to the needs of the faithful, Bishop Carroll read the letter given to him by Mitri with some interest. The Bishop of Hildesheim-Paderborn asked his fellow bishop to grant Father Brosius permission to travel with Herr Schmidt on his tour of the nation. It added details about this unusual European noble now sitting in his rooms, revealing much of his upbringing and confirming what Carroll recognized immediately. Demetrius Augustine Gallitzin was of the highest aristocratic lineage but was not some mindless fop fleeing the horrors of the French Revolution. Mitri had come to America of his own free will and perhaps for some divinely inspired purpose. The second letter, from Amalia, was more personal as she asked Carroll to assist her son in his struggle against "the two great enemies of his salvation, laziness and emptiness." Amalia also gave a promise of one hundred French pounds each year in perpetuity to the mission to which Father Brosius was assigned as a reward for his temporary service to her son.

Pleased with the added financial contribution and hopeful that the visit would benefit the Church, Bishop Carroll offered Mitri accommodations at the Sulpician Seminary of Baltimore, St. Mary's. The young prince responded with sincere gratitude and added resolutely that the place was appropriate because he was hopeful of becoming a priest, specifically for missionary duties. Bishop Carroll expressed his deep pleasure out of courtesy, but he had misgivings about the capacity of this nobleman to endure the numerous hardships faced by all of the priests in the wilderness and settlements of the young United States.

A consummate host and guide, Bishop Carroll took his guest on rides across much of the nearby countryside, exploring towns and cities. They went deep into the Maryland wilderness as well, and the prelate showed Mitri the rugged conditions of the area. He also gave him tours of the dilapidated chapels that served as centers for Catholic worship outside of the larger towns and cities. Above all, the bishop impressed upon the visitor the daily challenges faced by the Catholics in America, and taught him about the rampant anti-Catholicism that characterized so many in the new land.

The hardships, the dangers, and the social obstacles faced by the Church only spurred Mitri in his vocation, so Bishop Carroll opened another avenue of thought. He suggested that the priestly life was clearly one for Gallitzin, but would he not be better fitted to the priesthood in Europe, where his noble lineage, his knowledge of seven languages, and his family's connections would ensure him a high office in the Church? Mitri replied with a sincerity that no doubt touched Carroll's heart. The young man announced that for him there could be no service higher or nobler than laboring for the Christ in the frontiers of America.

Gallitzin was dazzled by wild America and knew almost immediately that he was called to the altars for this nation. While he left to his

Heavenly Father the particulars of his labors, he committed himself squarely to the American missions. This call was matched by two other practical considerations. First, service in the priesthood in the United States would keep him far removed from the potential troubles that might be directed at him by Russia and its disapproving government. Second, Amalia would have taken over his career and dominated his decisions in Europe. In America, he was Christ's alone. In America, he could demonstrate his loyalty and commitment on his own.

Convinced by such conversations and by prayers that Mitri was truly committed to the life of the priesthood, Bishop Carroll wrote to Father Nagot, the rector of St. Mary's Seminary on November, 5, 1792:

> Reverend and Most Honored Sir:
> Some time ago Augustine Smith, a scion of a Russian Family came to America with the German clergyman, Brosius. His sole intention was to travel and see this country, it being the desire of his parents, at least that of his military father, that his education might be developed by experience. On his arrival the young man adopted the name of Smith as you know, his family name being Gallitzin. He has been in your establishment for some time and you have been able to judge him for yourself. I am sending this to you as he wishes to remain here and enter the ecclesiastical state. His decision is to remain in your seminary to prepare himself for the ministry. Doubtless he will persevere, for he is pious and deliberate. His support will come from his parents, and I most heartily recommend him to you. He has no letters with him, but I am certain he is sincere and fit to be a Levite of the Church. His zeal and ardor should do much for religion here especially with the Germans. Much of the world that was with him when he came here has left, and he is remarkably devotional to our patroness. His talent is evident as you have noted and you may direct it to a good turn. I am with profound veneration reverend Sir.
> Your most obedient servant in Christ,
> J.Bp. of Baltimore

Thus, only eight days after arriving in the United States, Prince Demetrius Gallitzin, "Augustine Smith," enrolled in the recently formed Sulpician Seminary of Baltimore. In the face of the growing anti-Catholic oppression in Revolutionary France, Father Emery, the superior-general of the Sulpicians, had dispatched four Sulpician priests to Baltimore in 1791 to open a house of theological studies for priests and seminarians seeking safety from the Revolution. In keeping with the difficulties faced by the Church, the seminary struggled to survive as a refuge for war torn Europe. At the time Mitri enrolled there was only

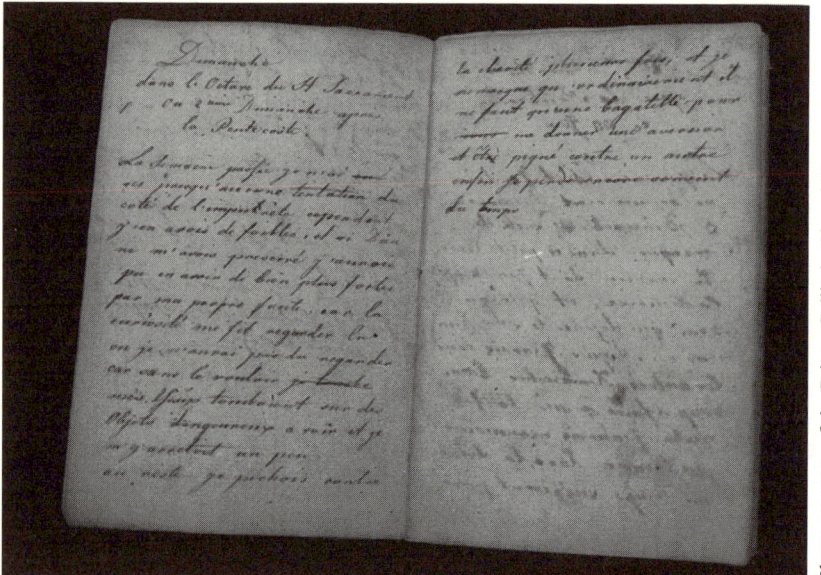

The personal diary of Demetrius Gallitzin.

Photo courtesy of the Prince Gallitzin Chapel House

one other student in the school — John de Montdesir, a young man who was ordained in 1795 but died a mere two years later from one of the diseases that flourished in the cities of the time. Bishop Carroll happily welcomed Mitri's arrival "as a great auspicious event," mindful as he was that he had only thirty-five priests to care for the faithful from the Atlantic to the Mississippi Valley.

The Sulpicians had been unable to find a house in Baltimore large enough for their needs and had settled in a building that had once been the One Mile Tavern, located on the outskirts of the town. Having established themselves, the Sulpicians next struggled to find seminarians, nearly closing at one time for want of students. Even after Mitri enrolled, he was never joined by large numbers of fellow seminarians. In the years that he studied for the priesthood, there were never more than five students. In the year before his ordination, 1794, there were only two students, and the year following there were none at all.

Through the next years, the seminary continued to endure hardships and chronic shortages of students. Early in the new century, as Napoleon Bonaparte stood as master of Europe and persecuted the Church, the Sulpician general master considered recalling all of his priests to bolster the ranks of the clergy on the continent. Bishop Carroll wrote to Father Emery, imploring him: "If it be necessary for me to bear the terrible trial of seeing a greater number of them depart, I implore you to leave here at least a germ which may produce fruit in the season decided by the Lord."

Carroll's optimism was echoed by Pope Pius VII. Even as he sat a prisoner of Napoleon at Fontainebleau just outside of Paris, the pontiff retained his firm and unshakable belief in the providence of the Church, both in Europe and across the globe. Upon reading Carroll's letter, he informed the Sulpician general, "My son, let it stand. Let the seminary stand. It will bear fruit in its own time." The pope was proven correct, for St. Mary's became one of the most successful and important seminaries in the western hemisphere, spearheading the training of priests for the cities and wilderness of America.

Mitri found the seminary exactly suited to his needs. While he delighted in its cherry trees and grounds, its starkness and rusticity were equally pleasing because they enforced a pastoral simplicity in his life and evoked many memories of his days in Amalia's retreat. This simplicity greatly aided him in his prayer life, so much so that he noted the fact in a diary that he kept throughout his early seminary days. The first entry read:

> The 12th of March. Examined my conscience. Considered particularly the good things I received from God, even from my birth. He gave me the great desire to please Him by being faithful to Him, by surrendering everything to Him. I made the resolution to spend a

half hour every Sunday meditating on what I might be continuing to offend God and to write every month in a few words the principal points of my relationship with God and His Holy Will.

My Confessor, to whom I give and owe entire obedience, consented to let me spend a half hour although I wanted to spend an hour on this meditation. I also promised to spend at least five minutes every day reading the New Testament.

His progress was encouraged by Father Nagot, who promoted his reading of the New Testament but discouraged Mitri's request to spend the daily half hour on his knees, suggesting instead a mere five minutes.

As his studies commenced, Mitri was still faced with the very grave problem of informing his parents of his vocation. He relied on advice from the Franciscan, Father Schnösenberg, back in Germany, who was kept fully appraised of Mitri's progress in the seminary. Amalia and the prince had to be prepared for the news. Mitri wrote his mother from St. Mary's informing her that he was lodging in a seminary. Subsequent letters began hinting at his long-term program of studies, including florid and enthusiastic descriptions of the missionary life. His hints earned him a rebuke from his mother that the longer he spent with priests the more he wrote like one.

A clearer indication of the direction Mitri was headed came from Bishop Carroll who wrote on December 13, 1792, to Amalia:

> That which I have learned of you, Madam, from Brosius and your son adds to my veneration for your virtues and binds me to interest myself still more in the welfare of Mr. Gallitzin. I believed the best thing I could do to respond to the confidence with which you have honored me was to place him here under my own eyes at the seminary which is being formed in the city. This establishment is well furnished with excellent professors; piety, the greatest of regularity, the love of study and seclusion are its characteristics. It is under the presidency of a French priest of the highest virtue,

Mr. Nagot, late first rector of St. Sulpice in Paris, but, by the changes in France, forced to seek asylum here. I have put your son in his hands for the direction of his conscience and surely he could not be better placed in order to respond to the views which Providence seems to have for him. I have the pleasure of telling you that, so far, his conduct is all that the virtuous and saintly Monica could desire in her dear Augustine and I am persuaded that his future conduct will not belie its present presages.

The truth emerged when a letter that Mitri had sent to Father Schnösenberg was read aloud to Amalia and her circle of friends. The Franciscan had forgotten his spectacles and gave the communication to Father Overberg, who innocently read Mitri's report on his studies. Amalia took the news with surprising calm, writing to her son and inquiring about his activities. He responded with the admission that he was studying theology at Georgetown College, adding his promise to write more soon. A second letter made his decision clear.

Amalia responded immediately. She gave her approval, but she reminded Mitri that upon his ordination he would be prohibited ever after from inheriting his father's titles and fortune. She also instructed him to write to his father, informing him that he was willing to surrender his inheritance. They agreed on this course of action but made no rapid move to inform the prince because they were wary of his reaction. Their concerns were perhaps justified, based upon the response given by some in Germany. The friends and relatives of Amalia, both Catholic and Protestant, were alarmed and skeptical about Demetrius's physical stamina and resolve. They blamed the chief villain in his apparent insanity the former Jesuits, including Bishop Carroll and Father Brosius. Amalia would have none of their criticism, announcing her pleasure with Mitri's decision.

Prince Dimitri was thus left temporarily unenlightened as to his son's seminary studies, although he was kept up to date on Mitri's travels throughout the United States. Bishop Carroll was in favor of the trips that were taken whenever Mitri had free days. These journeys, often shared with Father Brosius, were a vital learning experience and were also in keeping with the expressed desires of the prince.

One such trip, to the growing city of Philadelphia, brought Mitri into contact with the unique pastoral labors of the Church in the United States. An outbreak of yellow fever had claimed several thousand residents, including two valuable priests, Father Fleming and Bishop-elect Graessel, and Mitri was deeply moved by their example. These men had risked their lives every day to care for the sick and to give the sacraments to those in need, and he cited their example in later years in his apologetic writings.

A full account of the sights and events was forwarded to Prince Dimitri Alexeievitch, who wrote back to express his pleasure on January 28, 1794:

> I have duly received your last letter of October 1793. It was a source of real pleasure to me, not only because I learned from it that you are enjoying perfect health, but also because, so it seems to me, you are deriving profit from your travels. The descriptions which you give of the territory you passed through from Baltimore to Philadelphia show excellent observation, and I was extraordinarily interested in these accounts. I beg you to continue in this way until you return to us. Judging from the description, the climate of these regions is quite the same as Moscow, being subject to the same changes.

Soon after writing this letter, the prince received word from St. Petersburg that Mitri was expected to report for duty in the Izmailovsky Regiment within six months. It is probable that rumors had reached the court of Russia that young Gallitzin was becoming a devout Catholic, perhaps even contemplating the religious life. Time had run out for the young man.

Prince Dimitri was taken aback and proposed as a compromise that his son enter the diplomatic corps. Amalia was sternly opposed to both courses, naturally, pleading that Mitri was prospering and that, as a Catholic, he would not do well in the military or as a diplomat representing an Orthodox court. Unable to delay any further what he knew would be a source of terrible disappointment and pain for his father, Mitri wrote to him and told him the complete truth.

Prince Gallitzin greeted the news of Mitri's vocation as just yet another disaster in a series of recent bitter personal blows. He had been forced to leave the Netherlands and go to Berlin because of the very real threat of a French Revolutionary army storming the Hague. The prince also saw Russia refuse to march against the French. Instead, the aging Empress Catherine concerned herself with the partitioning of Poland with Prussia and Austria and then died on November 17, 1796. The succession of her emotionally unstable son, Paul, did not offer hope or cheer to the prince or anyone else. The new tsar's ideas were very different from his mother's, and her old favorites at court, Gallitzin included, found themselves in a precarious imperial atmosphere.

The prince was thus occupied with his own aristocratic career when Mitri's announcement arrived, and as a result he was far more receptive to Amalia's pleas for understanding. Actually, the prince, expressing a certain relief, reasoned that if Mitri had to be a priest, it was better that he should serve as a missionary or monk to prove his sincere desire to surrender all noble interests or ambition. He would never approve of Demetrius as a prelate in Europe because such a station would present him as a grasping aristocrat, a traitor to his family values. It would place him chronically in contact with his Russian relatives, and he would be a distressing reminder of the family's shame at the imperial court. His conciliatory frame of mind was clear in a letter he wrote to Amalia:

> True, he will never get my consent and approbation to enter the clerical state. But I pledge you my word that if I should see him again, I shall greet him in the best way possible. I shall not permit one harsh word to pass my lips, much less accost him with any show of anger or insult. I have already exhausted all of my arguments on him; it is for him now to undeceive me.

With this seemingly final hurdle passed, Mitri was free of his past and its complicated temporal obligations. He concentrated on his studies and watched as the day approached for his reception of minor orders and his diaconate. He received the former on September 23, 1794, and the latter on March 14, 1795. Four days later, on March 18, 1795,

Mitri was ordained a priest for the young nation of America by Bishop Carroll. Soon after, he joined the Sulpician Order as a testament to his gratitude to the congregation for his education, both intellectual and spiritual, at St. Mary's.

Young Demetrius Gallitzin had achieved his goal of ordination. Where his fall in the water had signaled his "second baptism," his ordination marked the final, ultimate embrace of the priestly life and the complete affirmation of his new existence and commitment to Christ. Perhaps emblematic of being a "new man" was the fact that while he had arrived in America as Augustine Schmidt, the official documents of his ordination state that he was ordained under the name Augustine Gallitzin, "otherwise known as Smith." Mitri also had the distinction of being the first priest to receive all of his orders, including ordination, in the United States. (He was not, however, the first man to be ordained a priest in an American ceremony. That distinction is held by Stephen Theodore Badin who was ordained on May 25, 1793, by Bishop Carroll, having arrived in the New World already a deacon.)

Chapter Four

The Mission Begins

> *"I went there [to Pennsylvania] to avoid the trustees and all the irregularities which they beget. In success, I had no other warrant than the building of something new, that could escape the routine of inveterate custom. Had I settled where the hand had already been put to the plough, my work may have been endangered, for it would have soon been assailed by the spirit of Protestantism."*
>
> D.A. Gallitzin

As an ordained priest laboring in the diocese of Baltimore, Mitri, now twenty-four years old, was a man under authority. While his classmate Jean de Montdesir was sent to teach philosophy and Latin at the academy in Georgetown, Mitri was still an enigma for Bishop Carroll. Both young priests were a treasure to the prelate and he planned to use both to the greatest possible value to the Church. Mitri's linguistic skills and his intelligence could have flourished in a teaching post. But Carroll had other ideas and intended to have Mitri preach to the sizable German population of Baltimore as an assistant in the mission at Conewago, Pennsylvania. Before Mitri began his pastoral duties, the bishop gave Mitri a vacation as a reward for his successful ordination and as a respite from his virtually ceaseless studies.

Mitri journeyed to Georgetown, where he spent Easter Holy Days along the vivid and spectacular shore of the Potomac, close to where the new nation's capital was being constructed; indeed, the cornerstone for the new city had been laid only in 1793. The planner of the city that was to be called "Washington" was the imaginative French Catholic architect, Pierre Charles L' Enfant, who resided during his labors with relatives of Bishop Carroll in the estate at Washington Manor. The new capital actually incorporated former Carroll holdings.

As Maryland was particularly stunning during that time of year, Mitri decided on an adventurous detour on his way home to Baltimore. Probably on horseback, he set out on a 150-mile tour around the picturesque peninsula that was formed by the Potomac and Chesapeake Bay. One of the places that he visited was Port Tobacco, a plantation located on an estuary on the Potomac. The area nurtured a large and devoted Catholic population that was still slowly, even hesitantly, emerging from many years of persecution under anti-Catholic penal laws. Two conspicuous and remarkable examples of Catholic vitality evident there were the new Carmelite convent and the Sulpician priest, Jean Baptiste David. The Carmelites, established in 1791 under Mother Bernardine Matthews, a native Marylander, were encouraged by Bishop Carroll. Instead of the traditional cloister of the European style, the nuns resided in separate log cabins while maintaining their rule of enclosure. Father David, working ceaselessly nearby, sought to strengthen the faith in the region. His missionary zeal earned Mitri's genuine regard.

Mitri found the spiritual vigor, the sea air, and the natural beauty of the Port Tobacco area invigorating, but while here he suffered a severe bout of flu. His poor health forced him to remain in Port Tobacco for the foreseeable future, and he received a letter from Bishop Carroll:

> Reverend and dear Sir,
> The arrival of Rev-Mr. Napier and your messenger yesterday evening relieved our minds from the uncertainty and many fears concerning you. You ought to have given us early notice of your delay and where you were. . . .
> How often you vary your projects gives me concern. . . .

Bishop Carroll also used this communication to turn down a proposal made by Mitri to remain as a permanent member of the mission at Port Tobacco. The prelate emphasized his need for Gallitzin's German speaking skills and his labors as an assistant to Father Brosius at Conewago.

Once his health improved, Mitri set out for Baltimore in obedience to the bishop. He took up residence at St. Mary's, enjoying the company of his teachers, although the nature of his life was quite different from his days as a seminarian. He spent time with Bishop Carroll and met many of the missionaries who were setting out to brave the dangers of the American wilderness. Mitri's primary assignment was to labor among the German Catholics of Baltimore, celebrating Mass, offering the sacraments, and giving numerous sermons. He saved some of his homilies, and these "Sermons given at Baltimore — 1795" were found among his papers after his death in 1840.

The first cemetery of the Alleghenies, with a rear view of the old St. Michael's Church, 1891.

Photo courtesy of the Prince Gallitzin Chapel House

Mitri's main area of concern was Conewago, Pennsylvania, where a mission was founded and headed by the talented former Jesuit, Father Pellentz (Bishop Carroll's vicar-general), and assisted by Father Brosius and Father Louis de Barth. Situated in a picturesque and fruitful valley in central Pennsylvania, Conewago had been launched as a mission on part of a tract of 10,501 acres initially given by Lord Baltimore to John Digges in 1727. The grant for the mission, called "Digges Choice," was provided in part by John Digges (a maternal uncle of Bishop Carroll), to the Society of Jesus, prior to the suppression of the order in 1774. It was an ideal location for a Catholic center, positioned on the Lancaster pike route between Philadelphia heading west and Digges Road, which meandered south toward Baltimore. Many Catholic families, mostly German-speaking, owned farms in the area, making the Conewago Valley perhaps the most devoutly Catholic region in the whole of Bishop Carroll's sprawling diocese.

Mitri traveled to Conewago in the company of Bishop Carroll in August, 1795. The mission church that was erected in 1787 still stands today in Conewago and was declared a minor basilica during the reign of Pope John XXIII. Dedicated to the Sacred Heart of Jesus, the stone edifice was the heart of a plantation that boasted a charming stream, a fulling mill, and a wool factory owned by Mr. Thomas Lilly. Lilly's sister Esther was married to Dudley Digges, the son of the famous John Digges.

Demetrius remained at Conewago when Bishop Carroll returned to Baltimore. Besides using his German to instruct and inspire local Catholics, Mitri assisted Fathers Pellentz and Brosius in what was termed "the circuit," the frequent missionary travels across the wilderness of the region that had no clearly delineated boundaries or jurisdictions for the outpost. The missionaries traveled as far as possible to labor among the faithful, at least as far as their endurance, geography, and mounts allowed. The Conewago priests thus had a mission territory that encompassed an area of some 20,000 square miles. They traveled to such distant settlements as Winchester, Virginia (100 miles away); Taneytown, Hagerstown, and Cumberland, Maryland; and most of southeastern Pennsylvania, as far as Huntington and Bedford counties. It is possible that trips were taken even as far as the Pittsburgh area, some 200 miles away.

As Mitri learned the long and tragic history of the Digges family, he was surprised to discover a distinct connection between the Digges line and Russia. Centuries before, an English gentleman, Sir Dudley Digges, had actually traveled to Russia, on a royal commission from the English crown. The infamous Tsar of Russia, Ivan IV, known as "the Terrible" (r. 1550-1584), found himself in dire need of funds, and he turned to England for assistance. Young King Edward VI, the son of Henry VIII, agreed to aid his fellow monarch, sending Sir Dudley with the borrowed funds. Unfortunately, not all of the money reached Moscow, as Sir Dudley was robbed by bandits near Riga, on the Baltic Sea. To make up for the loss, the redoubtable Englishman tried his hand at matchmaking, nearly arranging a marriage between Ivan the Terrible and an Englishwoman, Lady Mary Hastings.

Mitri met the latest generation of the landowning Digges family, Dudley Digges, a devout Catholic who had come into his inheritance while still a youth. His father, John Digges, was shot to death by Jacob Kitzmiller as Digges tried to push a group of Dutch squatters off land in the Digges Choice grant. As he lay dying, John Digges pleaded that his killer not be punished, leaving judgement to God instead.

This was the mission for which Mitri had long hungered. His love for the American wilderness deepened with each missionary trip, and the physical exertions were nothing in comparison to the joy he experienced on the trails in the forests and mountains as he journeyed to spread the faith. The work also brought him into contact with the new Americans, men and women who had fought for their independence. Mitri shared in their daily lives, in the cabins, on the farms, and in the crowded, often reeking and dirty taverns where he spent nights of rest and prayer at crossroads. For the Catholics to whom he ministered, Mitri celebrated Mass in barns and simple homes, heard confessions in kitchens and the open air, and helped to build chapels wherever local Catholics could afford to support them.

Still, he had to contend with the severe anti-Catholicism that was rampant throughout the new country. The Penal Laws instituted by the Colonies were still honored in spirit, even though freedom of religion had been officially declared. For their personal safety, most frontier or missionary priests dressed as Quakers or wore normal lay clothing. Hostile, even murderous bands of Protestant extremists might be encountered anywhere — along a country road, in a deserted forest or on a mountainside, in any village or tavern. Indeed, Father Brosius had only recently narrowly escaped murder at the hands of murderous Protestant assailants. Pursued by the riders, Brosius had ridden for his life and found safety — with death literally at his heels — at the farm owned by the Catholic James Stillinger, near Chambersburg, Pennsylvania.

Mitri was on his way to celebrate Mass when he had an encounter first-hand with anti-Catholicism. Somewhat uncertain about his bearings, he asked a passerby where he might find the Stillinger farm. The rider pointed him in the right direction and went on. A few minutes later, Mitri, hearing the rider calling to him, turned and watched as the stranger galloped to join him. In what the rider must have thought was an act of kindness, he suggested Mitri be careful because Stillinger was "a Papist."

As part of his work at Conewago, Mitri journeyed to Taneytown, Maryland, and spent time at St. Joseph's Church. Most of his flock at Conewago spoke German, but at Taneytown he found an English-speaking population. His time at St. Joseph's improved his English, but it also brought him into the sphere of trusteeism, a truly American threat to the Church based on Protestant traditions.

Taneytown was founded in 1762 by Raphael Taney, whose wife was Eleanor Digges, an aunt of Dudley Digges, Jr. Another notable family in the area was that of Michael McGuire, who, for a time, owned a tavern in Taneytown with a friend, Adam Goode. While they eventually settled in the Alleghenies, there were still McGuire descendants

Photo courtesy of the Sisters of St. Joseph, Baden, Pennsylvania

The vestments worn by Fr. Gallitzin and his sword. These were sent by his mother and were made from her wedding dress.

in the area when Father Augustine Smith — Mitri — arrived to minister in Taneytown as pastor.

The young priest spent only a short time in that farming community before the problem of trusteeism became evident. Protestant in origin, trusteeism was the practice of placing the parish in the hands of a board of parishioners, or trustees — many of whom were not even Catholic — invited on to the board for their supposed financial sense. These groups operated parishes as profit-making organizations, frequently treating donations and collections as mere fund-raising activities with the proceeds going to themselves. Even worse, the trustees took the position that the priest was a mere employee who could be rejected by them and whose decisions were subject to their veto.

In controlling the parish, the trustees found ways to demonstrate their superior rank over other, non-trustee Catholics in the parish, often through money-raising activities. Later in his life, Mitri related his personal experiences with his devoted assistant Father Lemcke, who recorded that while in Philadelphia, Mitri once had to celebrate Mass in a church whose trustees had rented out the basement to a wine merchant. Throughout the service, the church was filled with the din of "interminable rolling and banging, loud talk, and shouts."

In another parish, pew rental was practiced. Each pew had a door that remained locked until "rent" was paid for its use during Mass. Naturally, parishioners crowded themselves into rented pews and other pews were left empty. Those poor Catholics who couldn't afford the rent stood in the aisles, lingered at the back of the church, or gave up attending Mass entirely. This problem was widespread in Philadelphia and elsewhere, and posed a chronic challenge for Bishop Carroll.

Coming from the sophisticated courts of Europe, Mitri took a dim view of such flagrant defiance of lawful ecclesiastical authority. As he watched the trustees parade in their rights and privileges, he remembered the horrors of the French Revolution, where anarchy ruled the streets and preyed on the innocent. Mitri came into conflict with the trustees almost immediately.

Adhering to proper Church custom and law, he chose to ignore the trustees and to administer the church in Taneytown as he saw fit as its rightful pastor. The trustees were incensed, naturally, writing a letter of complaint to Bishop Carroll. The bishop urged them to be obedient to their pastor, but he then steered Mitri toward a course of moderation. The bishop suggested that he ease his ardor and use kindness and gentleness to win over his flock so that, in time, he would be able to guide them along the right path.

Mitri was committed to defending the rights of the Church and his bishop. He drew the line against the trustees whenever possible, alarming them and causing a stir each time. However, it was not long before all of the Catholic people of Taneytown came to have genuine respect and affection for their pastor. More important, the years that Mitri spent in Taneytown (when not out on the Conewago circuit) gave him confidence as a pastor, as well as experience in dealing with various types of parishioners, and the time to formulate in detail his own plans for the future.

The conflict with the trustees of Taneytown had a twofold influence on Mitri's work. First, he was able to stand as a bulwark against the heinous practice at a time when Bishop Carroll needed assistance in his wider struggle to bring order to his far-flung diocese. As a result, the bishop developed a profound trust and an appreciation for the young priest who demonstrated intense loyalty to the Church and to his bishop. The event marked, in many ways, a turning point in their relationship. Bishop Carroll had initially given the young priest only comfortable postings, still uncertain about his pastoral skills and his personal commitment. It became apparent that Father Gallitzin brought to his labors a profound awareness of the role of the Church in forging a moral, stable society. Mitri had heard the siren songs of the Enlightenment in France and had witnessed the chaos that ensued when humans believe they are masters of their temporal and eternal destinies. He had witnessed the pomp and pageantry of great, ancient empires, and he had seen grand armies march to bloody battles. To the priest, the strutting boasts of simple American trustees with their bullying ways were little more than parodies, ridiculous charades that had no place in the Church of Christ. Mitri would never tolerate or indulge the parish in oafish displays. His historical perspectives and spiritual insights won Bishop Carroll's complete trust.

His Taneytown experience also convinced the young priest to avoid the ridiculous interference of trustees and to forge a parish that would be free of their irregularities. He would have to travel far from the settled parishes of Maryland and Pennsylvania before he would find his pastoral Eden in the mountains of Pennsylvania. For four years, from 1795-1799, Mitri petitioned Bishop Carroll to give his blessing to the proposed new site where Mitri believed his labors were needed sorely and where he could give of himself absolutely as a priest. Mitri wanted to go to the Allegheny Mountains, to an idyllic site called the Clearfields.

Chapter Five

To the Clearfields

"Thus it was that on a spot in which, scarcely a year previous silence had reigned over vast solitudes, a prince, thenceforward cut off from every other country, had opened a new one to pilgrims from all nations, and that, from the wastes which echoed no sounds but the howling of the wild beast, welled up the divine song which spoke: 'Glory to God in the highest, and peace, on earth, to men of good will.'"

Account of Reverend Lemcke

The tradition relates that on an autumn evening in October, 1795, Father Mitri sat in the mission home in Conewago with Father Pellentz and Father Brosius, and another priest, Father de Barth. Their conversation was interrupted by a visitor who was greeted at the door by Brother Christopher Andrews. The brother entered the sitting room where the priests were conversing and announced that Mrs. Rachel Brown McGuire desired to speak with them on a matter of some urgency. Before he could finish, they were joined by Mrs. McGuire, who impressed upon the priests the importance of her mission by wasting no time on the niceties of being announced. Her purpose, she proclaimed, was to aid her neighbor, a Protestant woman, Mrs. Susan Barlow Burgoon, who was the wife of a Catholic, and lived far to the west on a ridge in the Alleghenies in a small community called "McGuire's Settlement." Mrs. Burgoon was deathly ill and desired to be baptized a Catholic before leaving the world.

Father Brosius had visited the central regions of Pennsylvania and the picturesque part of the Alleghenies she mentioned. In fact, Father Brosius had consecrated the cemetery in which Mrs. McGuire's husband, the well-known and respected Michael McGuire, had been bur-

The Alleghenies.

ied on November 17, 1793. Rather than return to the mountain colony himself, he proposed that Mitri go to McGuire's Settlement to do the honors. Father Brosius also recommended that Mrs. McGuire spend the night with her relatives in Taneytown and then set out in the morning to cover the 130 miles to the mountains and the deathbed of Mrs. Burgoon.

Mitri and Mrs. McGuire reportedly traveled four days along the wild trails of Pennsylvania, leaving behind the familiar communities around the Conewago mission as they headed for the first ridge of the Alleghenies. Following the Juniata River, Mitri and Mrs. McGuire made their way north to the fort and settlement called Huntingdon, the county seat, meaning that it boasted the symbol of civilization — a courthouse. They continued on, reaching the community of Frankstown (modern Hollidaysburg) before embarking on the Kittanning Path, an old Indian trail that connected the Juniata Path with the Allegheny River. Finally, they arrived at the ridge that is occupied today by the town of Gallitzin. The area was truly a wilderness, seemingly uninhabited, and stunning at that time of year as the leaves on the trees were turning red and gold and the first hint of winter was descending upon the night air.

It was evening when Mitri came to the cabin of the Burgoon family in McGuire's Settlement. He baptized Mrs. Burgoon, met and conversed with her family, and then spent a pleasant night in the nearby cabin owned by Luke McGuire, son of Mrs. McGuire. The following morning he offered Mass, probably paid another consoling visit to Mrs. Burgoon, who appears to have recovered from her illness, and took a long and increasingly loving look at the wilderness to which God and the priestly ministry had brought him.

The view from McGuire's Settlement took Mitri's breath away. He beheld a plateau covered in evergreen trees and vividly-colored hazel and oak trees complemented by meadows that only served to accentuate the sprawling ridges of the Alleghenies and the grandeur of the forests. Mitri learned that the name of this extensive tableland was the "Clearfields," derived from the fact that the meadows marked the only clearing in the forest for many miles in every direction. It was here that the local native American tribes had once set up camps: the Cherokee, Shawnee, and Delaware. The Indians were no longer part of the lovely scene, driven west by the coming of the Europeans or depleted in numbers by battles, incessant migrations, and the dread predations of the white man's incurable diseases. Now Clearfields was beautiful, fertile, and home to a dozen Catholic families, most of whom had arrived in the mountains with the encouragement and help of Michael McGuire.

McGuire had been one of the truly remarkable breed of early Americans who pushed the frontiers of the colonies and then the young United States ever westward, always in search of adventure, hunting grounds, and new lands. Born to a Catholic family in Maryland in 1717, McGuire eventually settled in Taneytown and became a partner with Adam Goode in a thriving tavern. McGuire was also a gifted hunter and woodsman, setting up a hunting camp on what became McGuire's Settlement as early as 1768. The woods were then filled with game, and McGuire enjoyed the natural splendors. The camp, situated near the borough of Chest Springs, received a somewhat official recognition by Pennsylvania map makers (who included it under the name "Captain McGuire's Camp" in 1793). This 1768 foray into what became Cambria County left a deep impression on McGuire, much as it did Mitri nearly three decades later.

At the start of the American Revolution in 1776, McGuire signed up with the Continental Army, serving initially in a Maryland company. Within a short time he was appointed an aide-de-camp to General Washington, a dangerous post that often required riding or charging into fire to carry important orders to a commander in the thick of battle. McGuire served as an aide throughout the war with distinction and valor. In recognition of his work, the Continental Congress granted him a fitting reward: two thousand acres of the Clearfields region. Captain McGuire was so pleased with the land that he moved his family there in 1787 and traded his share of the Taneytown tavern to Adam Goode in return for the parcel of land owned by Goode, located next to McGuire's new property.

The grave of Michael McGuire. (Photo courtesy of Mr. James Seiler.)

Other Catholic families followed McGuire's clan and purchased land in the Clearfields from McGuire's extensive holdings. Within a short time, McGuire's Settlement was established. It was a Catholic community in the middle of the wilderness; located about fifty miles north of the town of Bedford, the seat of Bedford County. McGuire had plans for the settlement, especially regarding its spiritual disposition. To encourage the presence of a priest, he set aside four hundred acres of land for the Church. This grant included provision for a graveyard, the cemetery in which he was buried in 1793.

The residents of the settlement were of the same basic pioneering, frontier stock as McGuire. They were aware of the dangers and demands of life in the wilderness, hunting for their provisions and carving out a life for themselves on their own terms. Where the fertile land permitted, many became bac country farmers. Individualistic and fiercely independent, they coveted their freedoms, but they also took pride in their faith. No better example of this commitment to the Church could be found than in the cabin of the McGuire family. There, on a table, proudly displayed, was the McGuire family Bible. The family's most treasured possession, the Bible had been one of the first Catholic Bibles published in America. Other area families had Bibles and prayer books from which they derived great spiritual sustenance even as they hoped for a priest to come to minister to them permanently. The infrequent visits, such as the one by Father Brosius in 1793, were appreciated, but a priest was needed to administer the sacraments and to give instruction to the families and children. Prior to Father Brosius, a priest named Louis Sibourd had come for a visit, writing in a note about the trip on December 13, 1794: "I received from Mrs. Rachel McGuire, a dollar for her part of the sum that ought to be spent in bringing a horse for the priest serving the parishes of Huntingdon, Sinking Valley, etc." He wrote again on June 6, 1795: "I have received the sum of sixteen dollars for my maintenance for six months."

    The individualistic tendencies of the inhabitants of western Pennsylvania were manifested in the Whiskey Rebellion of 1794, just one year before Mitri's arrival. Backcountry farmers in Pennsylvania regularly used their surplus grain supply to make whiskey, which they then sold, avoiding the tax on liquor imposed by Alexander Hamilton, Secretary of the Treasury. Hamilton hoped to raise additional revenue for the still young federal government through a tax on liquor. When the Pennsylvanians resisted the revenue agents sent out to collect the taxes, tensions mounted, climaxing in July, 1794, in an attack on the home of the regional tax inspector by an angry mob. President Washington ordered militia regiments mustered from four states to handle the matter, and an army of 13,000 men marched into western Pennsylvania. There were no military engagements, and the uprising melted away. Some of the leaders of the rebellion were tried, but the two convicted of treason eventually received presidential pardons. The whole business appalled Jeffersonian Republicans and left many Pennsylvanians embittered and mistrustful of outsiders.

The Whiskey Rebellion was still fresh in the memories of the inhabitants of western Pennsylvania when Mitri arrived to baptize Mrs. Burgoon. Nevertheless, he was received warmly by Luke McGuire and the other people of the settlement who welcomed him as a priest and as a traveler who had covered a great distance to bring the sacraments to someone in need.

For his part, Mitri was enchanted by the area and edified by the faith of the residents. It was clear to him that while land had been set aside by Michael McGuire for the Church, the community lacked many of the resources needed to support a full-time established parish. The people still deserved a parish, and a full-time priest, and Mitri resolved then and there that he would be their pastor. To confirm his commitment, he purchased with his own money 328 acres of land adjoining the many acres of the McGuires. The acres that were acquired by Mitri for 619 pounds and 10 shillings — according to him "twice what it should have been" — had been owned by William Holliday. Mitri then celebrated Mass, baptized several infants, took his leave of the newest Catholic in the settlement, Mrs. Burgoon, and set out toward the east to Conewago. Yet in his heart the images remained, and he not only understood the fullness of his priesthood, but he knew quite clearly the site of his ministerial labors.

As he returned to the Conewago mission, Mitri hoped that Bishop Carroll might appoint him to the distant Allegheny settlement. Of course the prelate had no intention of sending a twenty-five-year-old priest to such a dangerous and arduous spot, and he instructed Mitri to return to his regular duties. The next years were spent preaching to the Germans of Baltimore and in the often frustrating but ultimately valuable labors in Taneytown.

In the midst of his travels and pastoral endeavors, Mitri received a letter from his mother. She suggested that he must, by now, be tired and bored with the brutal conditions of the American wilderness. Additionally, she added, only by returning to Europe could he have any hope of being reconciled to his father and securing the inheritance that was his as a legal heir. Mitri's reply, written in 1799, read:

> You can be fully assured that I have no other will in life, and wish to have no other, than that of fulfilling God's will. I have no other will than to please God, to make

myself and my neighbors eternally happy. To attain this purpose, I am ready to renounce all that can please me in this world. You can be further assured that I find no lasting joy outside the activities of my calling, the commerce with God, the reading of spiritual books, etc., and that I could not be happy in any other lot than in my present one. This is my purpose, my deepest disposition, which I wish to bring before the Judgment Seat of God. Would to God I may carry it out properly so that I could feel more happiness and peace.

I am very uneasy in regards to my father and do not know what his present disposition towards me is. May it please God that he have a good one towards his own self, for then I should be quite content in regard to all else no matter what it might be. God may do with us as He will; I must go on with the course I have begun. I want to live and die as an Apostle of Jesus Christ and wish it were God's will that I might in addition die a martyr of faith and live with such good fortune as came to one of my colleagues on the eighth of September of this year. He died a victim of the infectious sickness which still rages at Baltimore, during which he did not cease to bring help to his fellow sufferers up until that last instant of his strength. I have been an instrument in the conversion of various Protestants, and had I rescued a single one of them from his path to destruction and brought that one into the Catholic Church, I would be more than abundantly repaid. More of this in my next letter.

I close with assurance that I ever remain with the deepest love and respect,
    Your Obedient, sincere Son,
    Augustinus, Sacerdos

A true priest emerges from the words of this letter — an individual tested by pastoral ministry and confirmed in his vocation. Mitri was no longer a pliable lad to be cajoled and prodded on his path to God. The letter probably caused mixed emotions in Amalia, and Mitri's declarations announced a distinct turning point in their relationship. She could rejoice because she had been more than successful in forging a spiritual human being who was committed to a single cause. At the same time, Amalia also felt a certain sadness. Yes, her son had entered the ranks of the priesthood, but he was now beyond her reach, secure in his role and his relationship to the Church and Almighty God. Her care and concern could close the miles between them with prayer and financial aid. But the daily trials and challenges facing Mitri in the young America were his alone to bear.

The colleague mentioned by Mitri in his letter was Father John Floyd, who had studied with him at St. Mary's Seminary. Father Floyd had been assigned to the chapel of St. Patrick's in Baltimore, a posting that included the spiritual care of the poor of Fell's Point in the port city. A popular and brilliant young priest, Father Floyd was infected fatally during an outbreak of yellow fever.

Even in the shadow of the growing metropolis of Baltimore, Mitri never lost sight of his distant mountain parish. He maintained communications with McGuire's Settlement through the friends and relatives of the McGuires still in Taneytown. Mitri even managed another visit to the settlement. A parishioner in Taneytown, Mr. Elder, headed west to prospect the region around the settlement and Mitri went with him. As it turned out, Elder fell in love with the place and decided to migrate there permanently.

Upon returning to Conewago, Mitri felt that the time was right to present the full scope of his aspirations to his bishop. His appeal had several notable points. First, he scarcely needed to remind Bishop Carroll of his troubles with the trustees of Taneytown; he was better suited to preaching among the backwoods people than the unruly and willful townsfolk with their notions of Protestant traditions. Furthermore, he already owned land in the Clearfields and was acquiring more land with the goal of selling it to Catholics arriving at McGuire's Settlement at a reduced price. Adding weight to his proposal was a petition signed by the families of McGuire's Settlement that Mitri be transferred to serve as their pastor.

All of these arguments were presented to Bishop Carroll at what proved to be a most opportune time, as the bishop was considering the pastoral needs of the Catholics in western Pennsylvania. The Catholic population was scattered across the western region of the state, and the likely center of activity — Pittsburgh — still only had a population of about 2,000 Catholics. The area couldn't support a priest, forcing Bishop Carroll to look somewhere else in western Philadelphia for a parish opening.

An alternate location under consideration was the mission called the Sportsman's Hall, situated some seventy miles west of McGuire's Settlement near Greensburg. The mission had been established by a Dutch Franciscan priest who had arrived from the West Indies with considerable wealth and had purchased the land known as "Sportsman's Hall." Upon his death the Franciscan bequeathed the cabin and three hundred acres to his successor, whom he presumed would be appointed by the Bishop of Baltimore. Unfortunately, the terms of the will were poorly worded, and an ambitious priest named Fromm came into possession of the Hall. Bishop Carroll could not permit such a challenge to his proper authority, nor could he give up such a useful property. A long and costly legal battle ensued, and while the diocese won the case, much was made in the Protestant press about the lack of Catholic unity. Once the land was in the appropriate possession of the diocese, Sportsman's Hall became valuable. In time it became the site of St. Vincent's Archabbey, Latrobe, and by 1799, it was being used by the reliable Reverend Peter Heilbron. Still, the Hall was relatively isolated, and Bishop Carroll preferred to have a parish in the midst of a thriving community, especially one assisted by private income.

The proposal given to him by Mitri met all of Bishop Carroll's requirements. Unlike the earlier time when Mitri returned from the settlement and hoped to become its pastor, Bishop Carroll had now come to trust the young priest and was pleased with his progress in Taneytown and on the Conewago circuit. He accordingly sent a letter to Mitri on March 1, 1799:

> Your request is granted. I readily consent to your proposal to take charge of the congregation detailed in your letter, and hope that you will have a house built on the land granted by Mr. McGuire and already settled, or if more convenient, on your own if you intend to keep it.

Mitri spent the next months making his preparations to depart Taneytown in August, a time chosen to avoid the dangers of travel during the harsh winter. He took to the task of his impending migration with his typical zeal and military discipline. A number of Catholics would be traveling with him, and he organized every detail until the caravan was ready to depart in excellent order. The wagons and the carriage, for Mrs. Anne Digges, Mrs. Elder, and Rachel McGuire and her mother, set out early one morning from Taneytown. With the ladies traveled members of other families, including the Dobsons, Alcorns, and the McGuires. They would go as far as McSherrey's farm near Martinsburg, Virginia, and there would await Mitri, who planned to depart by horse from Taneytown later in the day. Mitri used the delay to say a fond farewell to his parishioners. Despite his troubles with the trustees, he was respected and well-liked by the people. Two important farewells were made to Adam Goode, the tavern owner and long-time friend of the late Michael McGuire, and to Father Zocchi, Mitri's replacement in Taneytown. He then rode to McSherrey's farm. His personal belongings, including his most prized possessions, vestments, and other items needed to celebrate Mass during the journey

The chalice used by Fr. Gallitzin. The chalice is still used in Masses in the diocese of Altoona-Johnstown.

westward were entrusted to a two-horse prairie schooner and its two friendly assistants, a wagoner named Noel and a German named Feltz known for his talents as a singer. While sparse, Mitri's other possession were sufficient for his needs and included numerous books in assorted languages, a bed, a bureau, flour, coffee, a supply of altar wine, and a small altar.

After Mass and a festive meal, the travelers set out the next day from McSherrey's farm. Along the way to the Clearfields, Mitri planted flowers: cosmas in honor of Sts. Cosmas and Damian, and trillium in honor of the Holy Trinity. Further stops were made at Sinking Valley and Frankstown, and at last the familiar hills and cabins of Clearfields came into view. Mitri received a warm welcome from the Catholics of McGuire's Settlement, and he was eager to celebrate his first Mass for his new parishioners. The Eucharistic service was no doubt a great joy for Mitri, but each celebration reminded him of his most immediate and pressing need: a parish church.

The place Mitri chose for his chapel was on the land granted to the Church by Michael McGuire, on a slope some two miles from McGuire farm. It commanded a splendid view of the surrounding countryside and was ideal as a symbol of unity for the entire community. The church itself was built largely by Mitri's own hands, using white pine for its walls, covered with laurel and hemlock. It was small, deliberately so, given the size of his congregation. The date to which the residents looked forward with some enthusiasm was Christmas Eve, for Mitri would celebrate his first Christmas Mass in the chapel.

The event proved a memorable one. Candles made from beeswax adorned the altar, and the most ornate decorations possible, laurels and evergreen boughs added color and charm. From across the entire region, Mitri's congregation made its way to the log cabin church. Far more diverse and rugged than the parish members in Taneytown, the flock that claimed Mitri, "Father Smith," as its pastor was comprised of farmers, grizzled old soldiers, Indian traders, and women and children who donned whatever they felt was their best attire. Over the hills and through the forests, braving snow and wind, they came to the new church, dedicated to St. Michael (partly in honor of Michael McGuire), and were greeted by Mitri. Music and singing filled the cold night air with the voice of Herr Feltz taking the lead. The most distinctive voice was that of Mitri as he intoned the Latin of the Mass and joined in a rousing rendition of *Gloria in Excelsis Deo.* He was home at last, and he was experiencing the unique joy bestowed upon those rare individuals who have given up everything in order to carry the Good News of redemption into the wilderness.

The altar of the old St. Michael's Church, Loretto.

The sense of order and discipline that he would inculcate into his parish, and his lofty ideals and aspirations, were products of his ancient lineage and education. His commitment and generosity were gifts from his mother, Amalia, and her training. Mitri also brought the Americans the graces of his spiritual perception and his adamant loyalty to the tenets of the Church. He was fearless in the face of Protestant bigotry and petty quarrels among Catholics because he had been raised in the courts of Europe, where men and women wielded true power concerning life and death. Mitri brought as well a mind trained in rational thought and an intellect that understood the spiritual and social disasters caused by human pride and anger.

Above all, Demetrius Augustine Gallitzin — Reverend Augustine Smith — was a human being who understood the natural splendor of America as he cherished the unique opportunities awaiting the hardy citizens of the young, new country. He would live among the people of his parish for four decades, dedicating his entire being to their spiritual and temporal welfare as a pastor. His self-identity as their parish priest was clear from the parish registry. In one entry, he began to sign his name as Demetrius and then crossed it out. In its place and with a forceful hand he wrote *Augustine Smith, Parochus* ("Augustine Smith, Parish Priest"). Again, putting aside the rank and splendors of the past, Mitri declared himself an American clergyman, a simple servant of the Church, called into the New World for countless souls.

He greeted the new century while at work finishing his own small house next to the church and in the process of establishing himself in his new parish. A progress report that he sent to Bishop Carroll on February 9, 1800, states:

> My lord,
> Being just now returned from the backwoods, and hearing of James Driscoll's going to Baltimore, I cannot let this favorable opportunity slip to give your lordship some brief account of the state of that part of the spiritual vineyard entrusted to my care.
>
> Our church which was only begun in harvest, got finished fit for service the night before Christmas. It is about forty-four feet long by twenty-five feet wide, built of white pine logs, with a very good shingle roof. I kept service in it at Christmas for the first time, to the very great satisfaction of the congregation who seemed very much moved by the sight which they never beheld before. There is also a house built for me, sixteen feet by fourteen, besides a little kitchen and stable. I have now, thanks be to God, a little house of my own for the first time since I came to this country, and God grant that I may be able to keep it. The congregation consists at present of about forty families, but there is no end to the Catholics in all the settlements round about me. What will become of them all if we do not receive a new supply of priests, I do not know. I try as much as I can to persuade them to settle around me.

The report is a rather staid account of progress in his new posting, but his simple phrases demonstrate key elements of his ministry. He was still making missionary rounds in the region, seeking out the faithful far and wide, and he was centralizing the Catholic presence in that region of Pennsylvania. Noticeable in his writing is an understanding of the times in which he lived and the challenges that would face American Catholics because of traditions of intolerance.

What was not mentioned in the report was the solitary nature of his priestly life, an imperative for many mission priests in that era. That solitude would embrace Mitri in time, forming his spiritual life in the same way that the silence of ancient cloisters shaped the contemplatives. He was an apostle, called to the front line of the Church in any era of the world: the parish. To this apostolate Mitri brought honor, commitment, and a true sense of *noblesse oblige*. In his solitary ministry he was graced with the wisdom of the Cross, nurtured in prayer, and solidified in his personal sacrifices.

Chapter Six

Pastor of Loretto

> *"Let us have one single spot for our sum, one single dare wherein the true Catholic spirit can have room to grow and manifest itself, and it will leaven the whole country. Let us be careful what seeds we drop in the furrows of this rich land; let us keep the faith uncontaminated here; let us own one place wherein a man can live a hearty, vigorous, joyous-hearted Catholic life. Elsewhere the ground is choked with weeds that must be suffered to grow with the wheat until harvest time, that air thin, vitiated, foggy and enervating; let us keep the moral atmosphere, with God's help, as fresh and invigorating as that of our mountains."*
>
> Attributed to Father Gallitzin

Having opened St. Michael's parish officially with the Christmas Mass, Mitri was determined from the start to establish the Catholic faith in the Alleghenies as swiftly and as firmly as possible. This meant that each pastoral journey, each marriage, each baptism had to assume a pivotal importance in strengthening the faith.

Having his own church, small though it might have been, gave Mitri the parochial base that he needed for his ministry and assisted him in enduring the often bitter conditions of western Pennsylvania. The winters were especially harsh, and Mitri rode alone over ridges and through valleys in blizzards and ice storms without the promise of aid should he become injured or ill along the way. In fact, early on in his mission he received a lesson in the possible perils awaiting the unwary on these arduous treks. After visiting a parishioner, Mitri set out for home and soon lost his way in the cold and snow. With the prospect of finding his way to his church fast dwindling, Mitri hunkered down in the woods as best he could, tethering his horse to a tree. To his surprise, the light of dawn revealed that he had spent the night within actual sight of the chapel. After a few such excursions, he became familiar enough with the territory that such a mishap became quite rare. He also developed an inner sense of distance and time, and he recognized landmarks even in blizzards, an instinct that aided the hunters and trappers of the era.

That first year at St. Michael's also bought two happy events: a baptism and a marriage. On April 8, 1800, Joseph Bradley, infant son of Charles and Mary Bradley, was baptized by Mitri. It marked the first of more than three thousand baptisms performed by him over the next four decades. About the same time, he also united in matrimony Elizabeth Burgoon, daughter of Mrs. Burgoon whose illness had brought Mitri to the mountains and who had been his first convert, and Nicholas Cherry. Before long, the residents of McGuire's Settlement began to refer to Mitri as "Doctor," a token of respect for his special place in their lives.

On July 15, 1800, Mitri sent a second report to Bishop Carroll:

> The church I got built last August is very often almost full and will have to be enlarged in a couple of years. I live at my own cabin since Christmas last, although in a very poor style yet. . . . I had to begin in the woods, furnishing myself with everything necessary for housekeeping.

As he had done with the Conewago circuit and in Taneytown, Mitri went among his parishioners to learn of their needs. The settlement would benefit from mills and a tannery. Above all, it required new settlers. In keeping with Bishop Carroll's expectations for the parish, Mitri did not take a salary. Mitri secured money for additional land purchases, increasing his original three hundred acres with the aim of selling parcels to settlers. Slowly, Irish, German, and Swiss immigrants were making their way into the wilderness and found the available land around McGuire's Settlement that they could purchase from him. Such immigrants, of course, did not have ready funds, so Mitri sold them an acre of land for one dollar, in installments, despite the fact that he had originally acquired the property for four dollars an acre. He kept a small parcel to serve as his own farming land in order to

The fireplace in the chapel house.

provide vegetables for his table. The produce also brought him added money and supplied healthy food for the orphans who eventually came under his care. To give further support to the settlement, Mitri founded a gristmill, a tannery, and a sawmill. Some years later, the sawmill burned, taking with it $1,000 worth of valuable lumber.

 The creation of the tannery and the mills were only a foreshadowing of his more ambitious hopes for the new Catholic city in the mountains. Mitri had chosen his site carefully, making certain that the chapel would glisten in splendor in the surrounding mountains. He had planned for three hundred house lots along the two main streets, called St. Joseph's and St. Mary's. Through his own skills in engineering, and with the labors of the dedicated residents of the settlement, Mitri made the site a reality. He chose to honor the community by christening it Loretto, sometime around 1800 or 1803. This designation was a reflection of his devotion to the Virgin Mary and to the beloved shrine of Our Lady of Loreto, Italy, along the Adriatic. Mitri also recited the Litany of Loreto each morning with the Rosary, a devotion that he continued when traveling on his mission rounds.

 The inspiration for the adoption of the name was perhaps given by a small devotional book that had been published in Antwerp in 1605. The book contained numerous litanies — including that of Loreto —

and had the name "Dmitri Golitsyn" included on the first page. This collection of litanies eventually passed to the family of Dudley Digges, whom Mitri had known, and was discovered in the farmhouse once owned by Digges.

While working to establish the Catholic community and to provide the settlers with a further sense of commitment to America, Gallitzin applied for citizenship in the Huntingdon court. His request was granted in 1802, and, under the name Augustine Smith, he became a naturalized citizen of the United States. The new position bolstered Mitri's resolve in the face of growing homesickness and the entreaties of his mother that he return to Europe. A crisis concerning his stay in America developed in 1803.

Mitri had been away from his family and childhood friends for eleven years, since 1792, and while the years had been active and productive, he was still a child of Europe. He missed his former life, the stimulating influence and culture of the Old World that stood in sharp contrast to the rugged environment of the American frontier, especially the Alleghenies. Mitri took comfort from his books and his music, but the intellectual vigor that was so exciting in Europe was noticeably absent in the mountains. Adding to his discomfort, the letters from home from his mother and the Münster circle reminded him of lost intellectual pursuits. Amalia's friends sent letters also encouraging him to return. Mitri's struggle becomes apparent in a letter he sent to his mother in 1802:

> It seems to me as if I absolutely must see you once more in order to leave the world in peace. God knows what is best in this, and what would tend most to his honor, but according to all appearances it does not seem as it would soon be possible. The number of priests is becoming smaller instead of greater, and the number of Catholics is increasing. I know that you are entirely satisfied with God's will, far more than I am, and that you ask to see only on the other side of the grave in the bosom of the Heavenly Father. But it would do me no good to lie down at your feet, to bathe them with my tears, to receive your blessing, and hear from your own lips that you forgive me everything. I would rather have

this than all the treasures on earth. I feel as if the hand of God were heavy upon me, on account of my older disobedience and indifference to your admonitions. . . . One has so many temptations here that I should be glad to end my days in some place, where I should have no other responsibility than the care of my soul.

Mitri's close ties with Europe tempted him to go back to the continent, but they also enabled him to accomplish his many early achievements at Loretto through the financial and material gifts sent to him. Amalia was his mainstay. She did everything possible to keep her son supplied with money, promoting the same generosity from the Münster circle and the many aristocrats of her acquaintances across the continent. Gifts of money were not her only contribution. She sent him books, a watch, a clock, the long-lost "Adoration of the Magi" painting, and items that might assist him in his priestly duties. The most remarkable gift was the set of vestments made of exquisite lace from Amalia's own wedding dress.

Mitri relied heavily upon this financial and material support, spending extensively on Loretto from his own funds and incurring large debts in the anticipation and the full expectation that he would eventually come into his father's vast estate. While this hope was an unrealistic one because of his conversion and ordination, he trusted that somehow providence would provide. This was a holy spirit of hope that most often was justified throughout his life.

The question of his inheritance was also a matter of some importance to Mitri's father, who still harbored

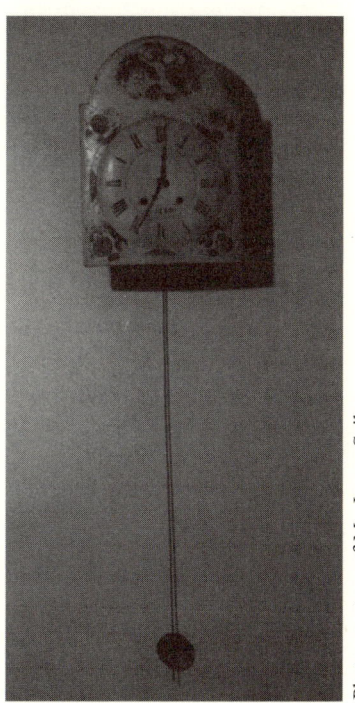

Fr. Gallitzin's clock, dated 1760, that Princess Amalia sent to her son from Europe. The clock is preserved today in the Prince Gallitzin Chapel House.

Photo courtesy of Mr. James Seiler

the desire that Mitri would return and settle the affair in a way that might yet satisfy the Russian government. The old prince wrote to his son:

> We are both [the prince and Amalia] quite advanced in years. Your mother, however, is weighed with infirmities, and I begin, especially since the past severe winter, to feel the burdens of my years. There is then no time to be lost, if you wish to see us again. . . . As I have already stated to you in all my letters, your return is absolutely necessary in order to arrange matters with regard to my estates in your sister's favor. Although you yourself have relinquished all claims by your choice of profession as well as your declarations to me, various formalities remain to be attended to, without which the property would go to side heirs.

Within a short time, Mitri received word that his father had died on March 16, 1803, in Brunswick, Germany, where he had been in solitary retirement. The old prince had just completed writing a letter to Amalia, in which he gave her assurance of his good health, when he suffered a hemorrhage. A mere three hours later he was dead.

Upon reading the letter, Mitri prayed even more earnestly for his father, and subsequently, he abandoned his bed and slept on the bare floor of his cabin, with a thick book serving as his pillow. A parishioner happened into the cabin and discovered the unusual sleeping arrangements. Mitri chastised the woman for intruding, both into his privacy and that of the rectory, but he explained that he had taken to the floor to perform penance. He felt obligated to assist his father's soul in overcoming the errors of the past. He could do nothing while the old prince lived, but he knew that there was still hope for his soul through prayer and atonement.

Soon after the death of the prince, Amalia urged her son to return to Europe to do everything possible to save his inheritance. Should he fail in this endeavor, the estate would pass to his cousins in Russia. This would mean an end to virtually all the money on which he relied, and the colony at Loretto would suffer as a result. Amalia added that should Mitri be unable to come, he should at least permit Amalia's three advisors (Fürstenberg, Stolberg, and Merfeldt) to make formal petition to the tsar on his behalf. Changes had occurred in Russian politics once again, and Amalia actually was hopeful at this time. The eccentric and unstable Tsar Paul had proven so incompetent in matters of government and foreign policy that a group of court leaders had staged a revolt in the palace at St. Petersburg in 1801 and assassinated him. His energetic successor, Tsar Alexander I, had a reputation for fairness and humanity. Nevertheless, the law of Russia was clear: Any nobleman who departed beyond the confines of the empire for reasons unrelated to trade was permitted to be gone for a period not to exceed five years. Failure to return would make the noble subject to seizure of property and permanent exile.

Equally aware of what was at stake, Bishop Carroll summoned Mitri to Baltimore and gave him permission to depart for Europe at the soonest possible moment. Father Nagot, rector of St. Mary's, was actually planning a trip to France to meet with his superiors, and Mitri would be most welcome company on the voyage.

Mitri desired to see his mother and sister, but such joyous reunions would come at a great price. He knew that with each passing day the pressure for him to remain on the continent would increase. Once permanently situated there at home, his noble family's connections, his experience, and his skills as a diplomat, linguist, and well-trained aristocrat would guarantee him a high position in the Church, perhaps even appointment to one of the sees in Germany or in the Holy Roman Empire. His mission in the New World would disappear into the blur of fond memories.

Mitri had convinced many men and women to migrate west by giving them the assurance he would be there as their spiritual guide. The families of Loretto and the vast surrounding region depended upon him not only for their spiritual but for their temporal welfare as well. Furthermore, there were the creditors who had loaned or given him considerable sums to build and expand the city on the mountainside. Should he abandon his mission, the Church's financial reputation would be damaged, making it difficult for the priests who followed to convince backers of their honor. Above all, Mitri was a citizen of the United States. His decision was made and his response sent:

> Whatever I might gain by a voyage to Europe in a temporal point of view cannot, in my estimation, be com-

pared with the loss of a single soul that might be occasioned by my absence.

Mitri understood that he was giving up any real chance of inheriting his father's estate by choosing to remain at Loretto. He was also denying himself the last opportunity of seeing his mother. Amalia, however, wrote:

> Whatever sorrow may have panged my motherly heart at the idea of renouncing a hope that a while seemed within reach, I owe it to truth to tell thee that thy letter has afforded me the greatest consolation that I can look for upon earth.

Amalia gave further affirmation of her acceptance of Mitri's decision by sending a supply of books, linens, rosaries, and even baby clothes for the newest arrivals at the settlement. She stayed in constant contact with her son and was also active in promoting the Church by encouraging missionaries to join her son in the wilderness of America. The rise of Napoleon Bonaparte as Emperor of France in 1804 had set off another round of wars and a greater oppression of the Church in lands under French control. The persecution of the Church, in particular the regulations that were instituted against the clergy, compelled many priests to leave Europe. This was often forbidden by law, so a network, of which Amalia was a dedicated member, was established to smuggle priests out of the Netherlands (under French control) to the United States.

One of the priests who escaped the Netherlands was Reverend Charles Nerinckx. A friend of Amalia, Father Nerinckx arrived in Baltimore and headed for Kentucky with Bishop Carroll's blessing. There he labored with considerable success in establishing the Church in that frontier area. Before his departure from Baltimore, the priest gave Bishop Carroll a gold watch that had belonged to Prince Dimitri Alexeievitch Gallitzin. It had been entrusted to Father Nerinckx by Amalia, with instructions to make certain that Mitri received it. Bishop Carroll had the watch forwarded immediately to the resolute pastor in the Alleghenies.

Mitri continued to derive great comfort from his mother, especially as he struggled with the hardships of parish life at Loretto. In the summer of 1806 he received word from his sister, Mimi, that Amalia was growing increasingly ill. Mitri knew that his mother did not have long to live, so he was probably not shocked to receive word from Bishop Carroll in November, 1806. The letter arrived decorated with a black border, and a second letter declared:

> The enclosed contains an account which will be very hurtful to your feelings, but full of comfort to your more deliberate and Christian feelings. It was enclosed to me in a letter from Count Stolberg who requests me to prepare you gradually for the intelligence conveyed by your sister's letter. Not being able, considering our distance from each other, to comply with this request, and knowing that after leaving your father, mother and kindred you will find the best motives present to your mind, I have determined to send you the letter without any other preparation than this cover to it. Since I received it, I have often recommended her myself, and prayed our other brethren recommend her to the mercy of God, though I entertain no doubt of her eternal felicity. It is not only on account of her relationship to you that I interest myself and desire others to interest themselves for her, but because she was the active, useful and earnest friend of religion in this diocese and earnestly sought to promote it.

Mimi's letter, dated April 28, 1806, stated that Amalia, "the dearest and most precious of mothers, now our guardian angel before God, fell gently asleep in the Lord," the day before at half past two in the morning. Assisted by Father Heilbron, who had come from the church at Sportsman's Hall, Mitri celebrated requiem Masses for his mother for three straight days.

As an added gesture of some importance, Mitri sent Bishop Carroll the gold watch that Father Nerinckx had brought him. The reason for making such a gift was simple in his own mind: Bishop Carroll, as he wrote to his ordinary, had been a father to him, more so even than Mitri's own "father in the flesh." No one was more deserving of the old prince's watch than Carroll.

The watch remained for a time in the possession of the Carroll family until it was given to Reverend Charles O. Rosensteil, then pastor of St. John Church, Forest Glen, Maryland. Rosensteil spent his final years in retirement with his sister, Mrs. Alma McGahan, who resided in Johnstown. In this way, Mitri's watch returned to the Alleghenies and ultimately came in to the possession of the diocese of Altoona-Johnstown where it is preserved today.

The death of Amalia could not have come at a worse time for Mitri. Not only did it deprive him of her spiritual and material support, it left him alone to deal with the difficulties of a group of scheming parishioners. His problem had been caused by a combination of Mitri's own priestly leadership and the monetary and personal ambitions of certain lay people.

While renowned for his charity and personal holiness, Mitri was also quite clear about his demands of proper decorum and behavior. In

Fr. Gallitzin's watch, originally owned by his father, was sent to the priest by his mother after the old prince's death in 1803.

Photo courtesy of Mr. James Seiler

performing his pastoral work, he spoke and preached with strength, conviction, and with the same straightforward and plain-spoken style that appealed to his rugged people. His sermons were direct, but they were also delivered with passion. Of his own talents as an orator, Mitri said that "he was glad that the same God who enabled an ass to speak, who enabled the illiterate to convert the universe, had enabled his ignorance to do something to the purpose in favor of Catholic cause." At times he would become so carried away that children and adults alike cried out in fright at his overwhelming spirit.

This energy and fire were also displayed in his leadership of the community. He regularly acted as a judge in disputes over ownership or grievances especially in the early days of the settlement. He punished children and adults alike for inappropriate behavior and discouraged excessive drinking among a flock that was fond of whiskey and beer, especially the Irish and German Catholics. However, Mitri was opposed to the temperance societies that sprang up in the early part of the 1800s, mainly because he saw them as tools of the Protestant churches. Instead, he declared the Catholic Church was its own temperance society.

Mitri's sternest demands upon his flock were reserved for the sacraments. Above all, he demanded proper behavior during the Mass. This was a natural concern given the wild conditions under which many of the parishioners lived. When they entered the doors of the chapel or attended one of the Masses celebrated in a visit house, Mitri expected them to display reverence and deep respect for the liturgy and the Eucharist. Silence was to be maintained at the start of the service, and no latecomers were allowed to enter after the Mass had started. For those in attendance, there was none of the pew rental customs that he had struggled against in Taneytown. The congregation was also strictly gathered; men sat on one side of the chapel and women on the other. Children were seated up front, close to the altar, where they could come to appreciate the wonders of the Mass more fully. Mitri could also keep an imperious eye on them throughout the services.

One particularly memorable event took place at Mass after one of the congregation married a Protestant. While the man's new wife was willing to accompany her husband to Mass, she declined to kneel at the appropriate time. Her refusal was noted by the others in attendance, and tension mounted as all awaited the inevitable reaction from Mitri. At last the moment came. Mitri turned to give Communion to the faithful. He strode up to the woman and said in a low voice, "Kneel down, woman, kneel down." She resisted and remained unmoving, prompting Mitri to bellow with intensity, "Woman, kneel down!" The woman relented and knelt down as Mitri's voice echoed in the wooden chapel. His reaction had a profound effect on her, for she came to Mitri six months later and took instructions to become a Catholic.

Naturally, Mitri's way of demanding obedience was not always well-received by all of his parishioners. The people of the region were generally devout, but they also took pride in their individuality, independence, and freedom. This sense of autonomy had been heightened by two events. The first was the decision by the Pennsylvania legislature to reapportion the prevailing boundaries of the counties. Huntingdon County lost much of its territory which was used to create a new county, Cambria County. With the change, the farmers and backwoodsmen were also able to gain political control of the county and build the future according to their own vision. The view of autonomy for local government was given added impetus in 1800 by the election of Thomas Jefferson as President. His administration emphasized the least amount of federal interference in the affairs of local government. As Mitri had been a supporter of the defeated Federalist Party, he lost a certain sway with some of his parishioners, especially those who tied political change to their view of him.

Mitri overcame virtually all of the difficulties with his flock through patience, love, forbearance, and forgiveness. There were, however, a number of Catholics in the community who came to perceive him as an obstacle to their ambitions and especially their profits. Their struggle with the priest lasted for years and reached a point at which Mitri's very life was at risk. This small group of malcontents was supported by assorted gossipmongers and Catholics who had taken offense with "Father Smith's" stern regulations.

The central figure in Mitri's troubles was a recent arrival in the United States, an Irish Catholic named E.V. James. After arriving from England, James settled in Lancaster, Pennsylvania, and used his skills as a speaker and rabble-rouser to become spokesman for the many Irish Catholics in the Lancaster area. His talents were used in a disagreement between Irish and German Catholics over the presence of the Irish pastor, Father Fitz-Simmons. The Germans ultimately triumphed, and Father Fitz-Simmons sailed away to England. Mitri heard of these problems and wrote to Bishop Carroll making the offer of welcoming the Irish of Lancaster. Rather than remain as a minority within a German Catholic community, many Lancaster Irish accepted the offer and moved to Loretto. Among them was E.V. James.

It was not long after his arrival in Loretto that James began complaining about what he thought was Mitri's ill-considered placement

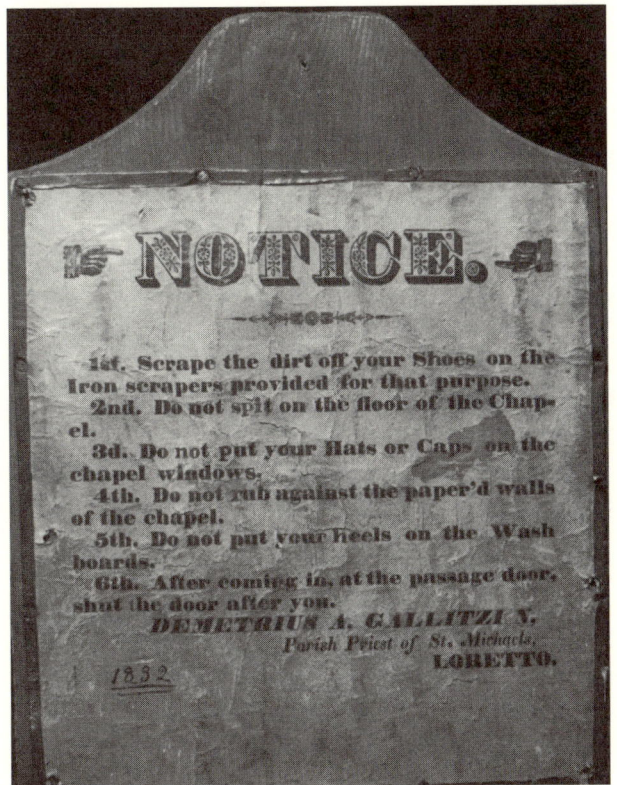

The notice placed in the Gallitzin Chapel stipulating the conduct expected of the parishioners.

of the town. Had the priest, according to James, established Loretto not on the mountain but on flatter, more accessible land, there would be greater traffic (and hence more opportunity for commerce) and perhaps the planned Northern Turnpike that was to connect Philadelphia and Pittsburgh might have gone past Loretto instead of Harrisburg and Huntingdon. James complained further that the county should have been situated in Loretto and not in the Protestant center of Ebensburg. It might have been Loretto had Mitri been more aggressive politically.

The clear commitment of Gallitzin to be impartial and to remain free of such political entanglements or ambitions, and his unwillingness to assist James in his ventures, left the Irishman angered and vindictive. James left Loretto and settled five miles away, where he bought four hundred acres of land along the line of the proposed highway. Calling his fledgling community Munster, James began to urge the people of the settlement to move away from what he called that dreadful place on the mountain and the intransigent German outsider of a priest.

At first Mitri ignored the birth of Munster, but as more and more residents of Loretto packed up and moved from the mountains, he finally realized the threat that James posed to the harmony of the community. As always, Mitri remained obedient to the laws of the Church and turned to Bishop Carroll for aid. After hearing a full report from him, Carroll sent a letter addressed to the parish. It was posted on the very doors of St. Michael's Church and notes subtly what he had given up to remain with the parish and its inhabitants.

> It seems to me necessary to acquaint my dear children, the faithful congregation of Clearfield, who are under the pastoral care of the Rev. Mr. Smith, that I am not unacquainted with the uneasiness which had prevailed for some time between the Reverend gentleman and some individuals of his congregation. Every inquiry that could be made at so great a distance has convinced me that Mr. Smith has, throughout this whole business, been influenced by the best motives of Christian charity and zeal for the welfare of those who were given to him in charge. He insists on nothing which can be objectionable. He is willing to act towards all persons of his flock with fatherly tenderness, and they ought therefore to give him assurances and proofs of their confidence and be willing to profit by his services. They should, moreover, be thankful too for undergoing so many hardships on their account and depriving himself, for God's and your sake, of many temporal advantages he might elsewhere have enjoyed.
>
> + J. C. Bishop of Baltimore

The letter from the bishop fulfilled a purpose, at least temporarily, to ease the strife. But Mitri was publicly ridiculed by James and his followers during a gathering that sank into a drunken revelry. Appalled at the excessive drinking, Mitri delivered a blistering sermon against drink during the Mass the following morning. Taking obvious and immediate insult, James and his cohorts refused to attend another Mass if it meant that they would be attacked by Father Smith. Mitri used the Mass the following Sunday to issue an apology to anyone who might have taken offense by his previous sermon.

The olive branch offered did nothing to mollify James. He continued his campaign against Mitri, whipping his followers into such a frenzy that they ambushed the hated pastor during a Sunday Mass. As Mitri prepared to begin the service, a group of James's troublemakers, armed with clubs, commanded the priest to leave or face the consequences. The flock begged him to depart rather than risk the danger, but Mitri met the challenge head-on. With full dignity and unnerving calm, he marched boldly to the altar, completed Devotions and began the Asperges, as though daring the now hesitant assailants to carry out their threat. As he perhaps understood the wavering of the gang, Mitri proclaimed:

> I now proceed to offer up the Holy Sacrifice of the Mass. Let no man dare to profane this church, or insult the Christ here present by word or movement . . . I tell you this — if any man raises hand or foot to take me from this altar, or interrupt my words this day, another day shall come when he will call for me, and I shall not be there.

With that announcement, Mitri continued with the Asperges and the remaining parts of the Mass. The service went on without further incident. While no other liturgies were threatened with interruption, Mitri felt uncomfortable enough that he decided to carry a pistol whenever journeying forth on his pastoral missions. He brandished the defensive weapon rather conspicuously, and it became the talk of the area. James seized upon it to lodge yet another complaint against Mitri to Bishop Carroll, going so far as to lead a delegation all the way to Baltimore.

Bishop Carroll resolved the matter with a customarily patient letter to his priest. In it he praised Mitri for his pastoral work and sought to give assurance to a number of parishioners who had written him stating "that I do not now entertain and hope never to have cause to entertain, a design of removing you from them."

The bishop added, however:

> It was very painful for me to read that threats denounced against you have induced you to be always armed. I dare not give any positive direction on such a subject, without investigating it myself with your feelings and seeing the dangers surrounding me as nearly as you do. But my general idea is that a pastor is best protected by the respect, love, and esteem of his parishioners and that possessing these it ought no be expected that any would be so desperate as to use violence toward you. Though Saint Paul enumerates his incessant dangers — In perils from my own nation, in perils from the gentiles, in perils in the wilderness, in perils from false brethren — we read not of him arming himself. . . . Your fortitude and sacrifices under so many trials excite my admiration. I cannot think without veneration on a person of your education, habits and former prospects for life, devoting himself to the painful services which employ you so entirely and expose you to the ingratitude with which your services are sometimes requited. . . .
>
>   + J. C. Bishop of Baltimore

A brief respite of the hostilities of James toward Smith followed, mainly because word had spread that the priest's mother, Countess Amalia, had died in April, 1806. Even Mitri's most bitter enemies called a truce and actually attended the requiem services held for Amalia. The genuinely sympathetic parishioners also raised money — fifty dollars — so that future Masses could be said in her memory.

But James was anxious to promote his original scheme of selling land at Munster. Unable to eliminate Mitri from the parish, he conceived another plan, suggesting that the many duties of the priest warranted the appointment of an assistant. It was not mere coincidence that he had such an assistant in mind, a Reverend Phelan, who was then serving in Bedford. Mitri saw through the plan and invited Father Phelan for a visit to Loretto. At the same time, he did suggest that it was not fair that Bedford should be deprived of its priest, even if Loretto was in dire need of additional clergy. Father Phelan grasped the situation instantly and declined the invitation.

Defeated again, James launched an even more ambitious endeavor against the priest. In his household, Mitri had a servant named Jacob Burgoon, a relative of the famous Mrs. Burgoon who had brought Mitri to the mountain. The Irishman convinced Burgoon to run for political office in the local elections and to request the priest's help in winning. As always, Mitri chose to remain entirely neutral, a decision that incensed Burgoon. The servant left the household of the pastor and, casting his future with James, he joined what became a renewed uproar over the priest. Mitri wrote to Burgoon a conciliatory letter.

That letter failed to reconcile Burgoon, and it had the additional effect of giving considerable encouragement to James and his supporters. They assumed incorrectly that Father Smith was on the verge of retreating. This was an illusion.

Seemingly in his worst possible position, Mitri surprised his enemies with his vigor and spiritual fire. He stood at the door of the church and refused entry to James and Burgoon and their fellow conspirators. Seeing the war against their priest as an attack on the dignity and rights of the Church, the majority of the people in Loretto and area sided with Mitri, initially as a quiet majority and finally as an increasingly vocal legion of supporters.

Undeterred, James took a gamble and tried to secure a final victory. He forged a set of accusatory affidavits and organized a petition of names requesting Bishop Carroll remove Father Smith from Loretto. James chose as the heart of his campaign the town of Greensburg, county seat of Westmoreland County. He could not keep word from leaking out about the petition, even from the distance of Greensburg. In response, Mitri's many followers drew up their own petition to counteract James and his minority. This was presented to Mitri, but he declined their aid.

On May 11, 1807, Mitri wrote a letter to Bishop Carroll to give him a full accounting. He explained that it was necessary to go directly to Greensburg and there make a complete appraisal of James's intentions. As his spiritual efforts had failed to reach James's heart — and that of Burgoon — it would probably be necessary to undertake a lawsuit against them and so bring the crisis, at last, to a head.

This plan was cut short by the arrival of word that James had already gone to Bishop Carroll and had won from him the dispatching of two priests from Baltimore to look into Mitri's conduct. Two concerns came to his mind when he heard the news. The first was the fact that Bishop Carroll had not informed him of the decision. The second was the distinct possibility that Jacob Burgoon would be eager to testify and, given his excessive anger and hostility, such testimony would be both tainted and dangerously unreliable. This final point Mitri included in a new letter to Bishop Carroll, adding that he looked forward to the investigation. He then set out for Greensburg, some eighty miles from Loretto.

The setting in Greensburg was a relatively familiar one to Mitri. Here was a well-developed community, and the educated, refined, and eloquent European was on firm ground in the legal setting. Armed both with the law and the spiritual strength of his pastoral ministry, Mitri presented his case resolutely and honestly to the investigating priests and testified in the civil suit that had been laid against him by Jacob Burgoon.

The once solid front against Mitri was already collapsing, as James's underhanded methods were finally being exposed. The most serious was the discovery by John and Mary Burgoon — onetime supporters of James — that their names had been signed to affidavits without their knowledge or approval. Their disappointment was compounded by regret when Mitri was forced on the basis of their affidavit to file a writ of scandal against them. John Burgoon went to Mitri and sought the priest's forgiveness and gave assurance that they had never been party to such a deceitful scheme. Mitri dropped his suit against the couple, and was now in a very strong position legally. As he had expected all along, he was exonerated completely and won the lawsuit. The priest was awarded $350 in damages, but he never did receive payment. A full letter of apology arrived from the now repentant and dishonored James. Dated July, 18, 1807, he wrote:

> The horror which I feel at the heinous crimes committed against your innocent character and the unsuspected faults of my heart, require me to humble myself before you and the congregation. I sincerely ask your pardon and that of the congregation in general. Of my Lord the Bishop of Baltimore, I ask pardon from an injured and offended God I implore forgiveness. I am

sincerely sorry from my heart for the many scandals I have committed by keeping bad company, suffering myself to be deluded in believing the most abominable lies against your innocence, joining in plots against your Reverence and being made the messenger of so many contaminated lies. . . .

Even in apparent victory, Mitri still had detractors and the remnant of the James conspiracy. The lingering hostility manifested itself in two ways. The first was in continuous slander, and the second was an outright act of violence against the priest. Demetrius Gallitzin had been known since his first days in America as Father Augustine Smith. His real name was known only to a precious few of the members of the Catholic community in the United States. Bishop Carroll was the one person most acquainted with his background. Mitri thus maintained the use of Father Smith with consistency. There was no deception intended. Rather, Mitri had desired not to draw attention to himself or to announce his noble lineage to a people who had just won their independence from a monarchy. Inevitably, some of the parish malcontents discovered he was an aristocrat of high birth. A whispered rumor swiftly spread that this nobleman priest, who had used an alias among them, must have some dark secret which caused him to leave Europe.

Mitri's answer to the rumors was simple. He made formal request of the Pennsylvania legislature to accept his name legally. The appeal had a number of practical considerations; deeds and formal acts by Father Smith — such as marriages and baptisms — needed formal recognition under Mitri's real name, Demetrius Gallitzin. By a special act of the Pennsylvania legislature on December 16, 1809, Father Augustine Smith was permitted to resume the use of his true name and all of his acts and duties as Father Smith were duly recognized as entirely legitimate. Within a short time, the full story of his life was commonly known and a newly found respect was paid to Father Gallitzin as his parishioners understood completely the extent of his sacrifices for them, including the temporal honors and wealth that he had surrendered in Europe to remain as their pastor.

Unfortunately, a group of malcontents made one last attempt at inflicting vengeance on the priest for all of the perceived injustices that he had caused them. They waited until Mitri was at home and then, when they were angry enough and drunk enough, they found the courage to launch a murderous attack upon him. At that moment, the defenseless priest was blessed by a titanic presence, a passerby named John Weakland. A mountain of a man who kept to himself and who was famous for his strength (it was reported that he had killed a bear with his bare hands), Weakland saw the danger facing his priest and jumped into action. As the attackers moved menacingly toward Mitri, Weakland fell upon them, wielding a rail of wood that he had easily torn from the fence that surrounded the pastor's house. The attackers panicked before the onslaught and ran for their lives.

Mitri was grateful to Weakland and supposedly later prophesied that one day a descendant of John would become a priest, and stand at the altar of St. Joseph's Church at Hart's Sleeping Place. The mission church, now the oldest existing church building in the diocese of Altoona-Johnstown, had been founded on the site used by a frontiersman named Hart as a resting spot along the Kittanning Path. The mission was blessed officially by Mitri on December 10, 1830. The foretold descendant of John Weakland, Father Bernard Weakland, was ordained and, in 1917, celebrated Mass at St. Joseph's, just as Mitri had prophesied. Only after the Mass was finished did Father Weakland learn that he had been the means by which Mitri's prophecy was to be fulfilled. As for John Weakland, he was buried originally at St. Augustine. Years later, his remains were

The John Weakland window in St. Joseph's Church.

Photo courtesy of Fr. Tim Stein, *The Catholic Register*

transferred to the cemetery of St. Joseph. When the body was exhumed, it was discovered that his right arm, the limb that had wielded the fence post in defense of Father Demetrius Gallitzin, was preserved incorrupt.

Though the conflict with his detractors appeared resolved, Mitri knew that there were still many challenges and obstacles to be faced and overcome. The trials of the last years, including his mother's death and the opposition of James as well as the daily struggles of being pastor in the wilderness, took their toll. This was revealed in the letter Mitri sent to Bishop Carroll shortly after his triumph over James and Burgoon. Dated September 2, 1807, it read:

> My Lord:
> With a feeble and trembling hand, and a sorrowful heart, full of the deepest and blackest melancholy, I take up the pen to give myself the comfort and consolation of addressing a few lines to Your Lordship. I am hardly recovered from a severe spell of sickness which attacked me at Greensburgh [sic], and which has left me so weak that I can scarcely crawl about, and have not been able to begin to say Mass again. Rev. Mr. Heilbron will be here to-morrow and stay with me a few weeks, until I can gain strength sufficiently to discharge my duty. Permit me to implore your patience, and to beg of your Lordship to administer all the consolation your charity will suggest to my poor broken and sorely afflicted heart. My constitution being weak, and my heart too susceptible of deep impressions from disappointments, losses, etc., I have been wonderfully low this great while, and I begin seriously to apprehend that my days will not be very long. I can better feel than describe the gloomy and melancholy state of my mind, especially since the death of my mother. The remembrance of former times, her tender affection to me, her last dying expressions concerning me, my own solitary situation in the wilderness of the Alleghany [sic], my sufferings and persecutions here, conspire to overwhelm me with sorrow and melancholy. O my dear

Lord! for God's sake send me a companion, a priest, to help and assist me, for my heart is ready to break. If you have one who does not know a word of English, for my comfort and consolation — a good virtuous clergyman — a friend to help me bear the burden.

Chapter Seven

Temporal Debts

> "For more than thirty years this venerable man [Father Demetrius Gallitzin] has chosen the summit of the Allegheny mountains for the center of his mission; from hence he has gone out from time to time to give the succor of religion to Catholics scattered over an immense territory.... Many Protestants have followed his example renouncing the errors of sects in which they have been educated; and Catholics have come from all sides to entrust themselves to the paternal care of a protector whose humble and pure life excites them to the exercise of evangelical virtues."
>
> Bishop Francis Patrick Kenrick, in a letter to the Society for the Propagation of the Faith (1834)

The resolution of his troubles with the flock of Cambria County permitted Mitri to concentrate on another vexing problem, his personal finances. Since his first days in America, he had relied heavily upon the financial support of his parents, especially his mother. His post in the Alleghenies was an exceedingly demanding one in terms of money, and Mitri had to borrow heavily from creditors in Philadelphia and elsewhere to fund his many charitable endeavors. The repayment of the capital would be nearly impossible from Mitri's perspective. Indeed, by 1809 his debt had reached $20,000. He was able to pay the interest through the generous gifts from his mother, but her death in 1806 meant that no further money could be expected from that perpetually beneficent supporter.

While Mitri had acknowledged the loss of his inheritance back in 1803, when he chose not to return to Europe and fight for his rights following the death of his father his mother's agents had continued the effort on his behalf. Baron von Fürstenberg, Count Frederick Leopold de Stolberg, and Count Clemens August de Merveldt had made every attempt to convince the Russian government that Mitri should inherit his father's vast estate, the laws of the empire notwithstanding. The letter from these agents read:

> The question concerning you and the princess's, your sister's claim to your father's property, is so determined by the Senate of St. Petersburg that you, dearest Prince, in consequence of your having embraced the Catholic faith and the clerical profession etc., cannot be admitted to the possession of your deceased father's property, and that therefore your sister, the Princess, is to be considered the sole heiress to the said estate, and is to be put in possession of the said same. The Council of the State has given the same decision, and the Emperor, by his sanction, has given the sentence the force of law.
>
> The Princess has, by the laws of Russia, perfect control over the income, but cannot give the property away. However, she is at liberty to sell it, and to dispose of the money arising from the sale. You see, then, dearest Prince, that you are only nominally included. . . . We, therefore, congratulate you on the happy issue of this business, without minding the killing letter of law; as in this case the spirit of justice and charity makes up for the loss of you.

Seemingly more good news arrived from Mimi. She wrote:

> I need not repeat to you that you may be perfectly easy if we only receive the property. Whether under your name or mine, makes no difference amongst us; I shall divide with you faithfully, as I am certain that you would do with me. Such was the will of our deceased father, and of our dearest mother; and such also shall

be the desire of my affectionate love and devotedness toward you, my dearest brother.

These developments could not have come at a better time. He was facing the grim prospect of financial ruin should he default on his loans, with severe ramifications for the many Catholics of Loretto who had trusted him with their lives. To minimize the impending damage and to spare his religious companions, Mitri resigned from the Sulpicians, of which he had been a member since 1795.

Meeting the obligations with energy, Mitri doubled his efforts at selling off his own lands and raised more money by acting as a land agent for the heirs of Henry Drinker, a Quaker financier. The priest sold plots of land in Somerset and Cambria Counties and received a generous commission for his efforts. Unfortunately, Mitri was required to travel and spend time in this task. He felt such efforts, however, deprived the faithful in his care, especially given the time he needed to operate the school and orphanage and the more mundane endeavors such as the mills and tannery.

A logical answer was to have an assistant priest take up a part of his burden. The conditions were now right for an assistant pastor, especially since Mitri did not have to worry about a priest arriving as an agent of some plot to undermine his authority. Unfortunately, the ongoing Napoleonic Wars, in which the French Emperor was winning battle after battle against most of Europe and tightening his control over the Church, made attracting priests even more difficult in the United States than in the bleak days of the French Revolution. Bishop Carroll did find at least one priest who might be able to assist Mitri, and the bishop communicated the news to the priest in late 1807. Mitri replied on December 3, 1807:

> My Lord . . .
> Your favor of November 20 was handed to me by Mr. Gill last night after Mass and gave me a great deal of comfort. I am so exceedingly fatigued from walking about fifty miles since last Monday through rocks and mire to visit the sick (my riding horse having been lost) that I am obliged to confine myself to a very few words. . . . In answer to your Lordship's proposal . . . I

shall only desire that I think myself in duty bound (and that for several reasons) to accept your proposal, provided your Lordship thinks it probable that the said clergyman is not likely to give any more scandal in the way you mention. From what little experience I have, it appears to me that abstinence from spiritous liquor is the only sure way of breaking a habit of that kind, and as I never keep any kind of liquor, nor drink anything than water or milk, he will have a fine chance of curing. . . .

As the letter states rather clearly, a priest with a drinking problem was not an effective solution for Mitri; however, the proposed new assistant failed to arrive on the mountain. Mitri was left to carry on his duties alone, and he dealt with his worsening financial situation as best he could.

How severe his economic straits had become was driven home when he was informed of a bank deficit involving his mother. She had sent a check in the amount of $400 to Mitri which was drawn from the Hamburg bank of Vogt and cashed by the Philadelphia bank of Laurent and Lang. When Laurent and Lang sent the check to Vogt for reimbursement, the Americans were informed that no such funds had been deposited. The Philadelphia bankers naturally demanded immediate recompense from Gallitzin. Serious trouble was avoided only by a hastily arranged loan that was given by Baltimore merchants with the timely intervention of Bishop Carroll.

There was thus much joy from his sister's letter, so much so that Mitri pledged a very large donation to Bishop Carroll for the new cathedral in Baltimore. Most of the remaining anticipated money he devoted not to his debts but closer to home — Loretto and its people. Even his increasingly clamoring creditors were mollified by word of his impending inheritance. As had been the case throughout the previous years, creditors loaned him large amounts of money merely because of his illustrious family and presumed wealthy associations. Now, with the money supposedly on the way, even more creditors were willing to take a risk on the aristocratic priest. Very soon, his debts had doubled in size.

The new money was not wasted, going directly to the Catholic community of the Alleghenies. In order to accommodate the growing congregation in Loretto, Mitri supervised the rebuilding of St. Michael's to twice its original size. His own house was enlarged to be able to care for more orphans, and a large storage barn was built to house what Mitri hoped would be a profitable venture in grain.

Mitri was able to send a report to Bishop Carroll on the present state of affairs. He was even pleased to note that the Irish — whom he frequently found to be lethargic in the fulfillment of their obligations — were proving remarkably faithful: "... even a good many of the Irish frequent the sacraments and present edifying principles of conduct. Some Protestants are also opening their eyes; last month I took a whole family into the Church, I venture to assert that many more would follow their example of our own members."

No sooner did Mitri give this optimistic report to Bishop Carroll than a new letter arrived from his sister. Mimi had journeyed to Russia in anticipation of receiving the promised inheritance and suddenly found herself faced with delays and obstructions from the imperial officials. Time had passed, and she had to spend the equivalent of $8,000 in lawyer fees and living expenses before giving up and returning home with nothing. The only piece of good news from Mimi was her success in borrowing a meager five thousand rubles in St. Petersburg — against the estate. This she had sent to the new Russian consul to the United States, a Mr. Daschkoff who was soon to arrive in Philadelphia.

Mitri wrote to Daschkoff to ask about the promised funds. After a long delay, Daschkoff sent a reply in which he denied ever receiving funds from Mimi or her agents. The communication was a disaster for Mitri as a number of his creditors were unwilling to wait any longer for their money. Mitri had no choice but to go at once to Philadelphia. His plan was to meet with Daschkoff and, if the consul failed to give an advance on the amount, Mitri would make direct appeal to Catholic leaders in the city. The priest didn't even have the funds to make the trip, and was forced to ask several parishioners for the cash.

As his effort to acquire funds from the consul met with no success, Mitri relied on his host, a lawyer named Mr. Carrell to give him time to make the rounds of the local Catholics. Once more the priest faced bitter disappointment and very nearly collapsed from exhaustion and despair. Instead, he returned to his prayers and made a small offering to God from what was left of his funds. Immediately after, five wealthy businessmen arrived (two of them were not even Catholic) and gave to Mitri $2,000, the very amount he needed. Without delay, Mitri set out for Huntingdon, paying his debts with only days before the creditors were to launch proceedings against him. Having been saved by Philadelphia businessmen, Mitri celebrated Mass with special joy. Only days later, a new batch of creditors informed him of their demands of payment of over $400 for money loaned from Baltimore. Mitri succeeded once more in raising the money, against impossible odds.

Stories are often repeated about Mitri's finding needed money at dark moments. In one such story, Mitri was sitting in his house one cold and snowy evening pondering his problems when he heard a knock on the door. A guest, who barely attracted the priest's attention, stepped into the light of the warm hearth fire. The stranger's coat was completely dry, and he spoke with calm and assurance, telling Mitri, "God has never abandoned you before. Why should you lose trust in him now?" He then departed hurriedly. When Mitri recovered from his surprise, he noticed that the stranger had left behind a wallet. There was no one to be seen, however, nor were there any tracks at all in the snow. When Mitri opened the wallet, he found inside $400, the exact amount he needed at the time.

The next year passed with Mitri continuing to amass large debts in his efforts to expand the parish buildings and care for souls. He regularly sold plots of land at a loss to the poor immigrants who arrived in Pennsylvania and was swindled by dishonest farmers who manipulated his sincere desire to help them.

Mitri felt a definite optimism for his planned business ventures because of the current economic conditions. The Napoleonic Wars were devastating much of Europe and, in 1812, the United States declared war on England. The effect of this declaration curtailed much of the nation's trade with Europe and drove up prices for products manufactured or harvested in the western regions of America. Western Philadelphia prospered, and Mitri sought to put the good economic times to use for his parishioners.

He organized a village store where the parishioners would be able to find luxury items and necessities brought all the way from Baltimore. As most of his parishioners did not always use cash, Mitri planned to use barter methods; parishioners could trade their own goods for products. One of the most common of these local products was wood, so Mitri borrowed money and built a sawmill. The sawmill burned down, however, and the man who was supposed to take the cart to Baltimore returned empty-handed. He had spent the funds in taverns, leaving Mitri disappointed but, as ever, patiently forgiving.

As the years passed, Mitri continued to labor alone in the mountains, balancing the great obligations of being a pastor with operating his own businesses and deepening his spiritual life. His simple, ascetic way of life made Mitri capable of devoting virtually all of his funds to his debts and to his parishioners. No better example of this is evident than that of his proud dedication in 1817 of the second church at Loretto to accommodate the still increasing parish members.

But debts remained a severe burden for the priest. Finally Mimi succeeded in gaining their rightful inheritance, but she delivered a tremendous blow — in 1819, at the age of forty-eight, she had chosen to marry a nobleman. Her husband, Prince Altgraf Franz von Salm-Reifferscheid-Krautheim, became an immediate obstacle to Mitri receiving his fortune, both because of his obvious presence in Mimi's life and because of his own large debts and rather irresponsible lifestyle. Mimi assured her brother that she was still in full control of the property. Sadly, Mimi's assurances could not be verified. While she was able to send money from time to time, her husband's financial missteps, his gambling debts, and his profligate lifestyle soon consumed Mimi's fortune.

The one genuinely bright moment in the new arrangement followed upon Mimi's letter. A voice from Mitri's distant past, Bernard Overberg, wrote that he was sending to Mitri via his sister and her new husband the sum of $20,000. This enormous amount had come from the sale of the Greek carvings which had been bequeathed by the old family friend Hemsterhuis to Amalia. In turn, she bequeathed the magnificent carving to Overberg with the intention that they be used for charitable purposes. Once put up for sale, the carvings were acquired by another family friend, Mitri's old boyhood friend, the Prince of Orange — who was now King of the Netherlands. The aim of the ruler — who was not Catholic — was simple. He wanted to aid his friend in his missionary endeavors.

As always seemed to be the case, the grand news was not followed by the promised money. After two years of waiting, Mitri wrote a letter to his sister imploring her to release the funds. To give added weight to his appeal, he sent a second note to Count Merfeldt, the sole surviving executor of Amalia's estate. At last the letters had their effect, and the Prince of Salm forwarded a check for $11,000 in 1823. Mimi promised to send the remaining $9,000 within a month, but the funds never arrived.

Mitri received the available money with a great sense of relief as his debts had once again been pressing, and his creditors were eager for repayment. A grander project of fund-raising for debt relief was necessary, and an ideal place to start was with the Russian ambassador. Armed with a letter of introduction from the holy Archbishop Maréchal (who was then archbishop of Baltimore, in succession to Archbishop John Carroll), Mitri presented himself to Baron Tuyll, a Holland-born diplomat in the service of Russia who had arrived on the same boat as Archbishop Maréchal. The baron was exceedingly friendly, suggesting that Mitri make direct appeal to Tsar Alexander I. The priest was clearly in need of money as the nine thousand had not been sent, so the ambassador gave him a suit of clothes and a bond of $5,000.

Both the clothes and money were deeply appreciated, especially as Mitri was faced with an increasingly desperate debt problem. On December 13, 1823, Mimi, Mitri's beloved sister, died, leaving all of the property to her husband, the Prince of Salm. Mimi requested in her will that he pay Mitri his due money and a share of her estate, but only after her husband had disposed of his own massive debts and obligations. Such was the prince's own need for money — from gambling and ill-considered investments — that Mitri had no hope of seeing a penny of the estate for which he had prayed and hoped.

For many years Mitri had managed to placate his creditors with the sincere promise that his own inheritance would eventually find its way to him. Mimi's passing ended this possibility, and the long patient creditors at last demanded payment in full. To solve this latest, and most serious, dilemma, Mitri set out for the east with great vigor. He first wrote a carefully worded and eloquent letter of appeal (penned in the third person) that detailed his predicament, the worthy circumstances of his having acquired debts, and his desire to be free of the financial obligations.

Mitri arrived in Baltimore in November, 1827, and met with Charles Carroll of Carrolltown, the cousin of John Carroll and the last surviving signer of the Declaration of Independence. One of the great Catholics from the era of the American Revolution, Charles Carroll was happy to help, giving the priest $100. Mitri next went to Washington for a potentially rewarding dinner with Baron Tuyll. The meal, convened in Mitri's honor, included the ambassadors of Portugal and the Netherlands; Peter Force, the mayor of Washington; James Buchanan, later U.S. envoy to Russia and President of the United States; and Henry Clay, one of America's greatest statesmen. Mitri wrote of the remarkable meal in a letter to R. B. McCabe, Esq.:

> After dinner some smoked cigars, and for the accommodations a lighted candle was placed on the table. I chanced to sit near the candle and noticed the Russian ambassador rolling up a paper very carefully to make a light.
>
> My eyes involuntarily followed his hand till the paper was put to candle. It was my bond for five thousand dollars he was burning. When I spoke to him on the subject, which I did at the first opportunity, he declared it settled. Nor would he hear any more from me about it.

More good news greeted Mitri upon his return to Baltimore. Cardinal Bartolomeo Cappellari, then prefect, or head, of the Congregation for the Propagation of the Faith in Rome had sent Mitri $200. The cardinal praised Mitri's many sacrifices on behalf of the faith and also considered him an excellent example of the project to heal the centuries-old schism that existed between the Orthodox and Catholic Churches. The gift had an added historical interest, for Cardinal Cappellari was elected Pope Gregory XVI in 1831, serving until 1846 and promoting the missions throughout his reign.

Baron Tuyll's generosity, and that of Cappellari and others, was still not enough to make a dent in the priest's debts. Matters reached a breaking point in 1828 when a group of creditors received an injunction and sent a sheriff to tack a sign on Mitri's house announcing that the property would be auctioned off to pay long-standing debts.

Having exhausted all other avenues, Mitri had no choice but to turn to the very Catholics whom he ministered, in particular the camps of Irish and German workers who had made their way to western Pennsylvania to build the canal system that would link the eastern region of the United States with the Mississippi Valley. The workers were regularly housed near Loretto and had been given a special welcome by Father Gallitzin, who cared for their spiritual needs and did his best to alleviate their many temporal needs and wants. The Irish were paid only a pittance and lived in camps that were squalid and lacked even the basics of sanitation.

With tears in his eyes and a heavy heart, Mitri addressed them about his need, sharing with them his anguish that his work was in danger. To his surprise, the poor laborers, both Catholics and Protestants, raised money for him in the camp. In a Sunday Mass celebrated in a camp virtually resting in huge gravel piles of the canal still under construction, Mitri preached but did not mention the subject of money. But word had spread among the workers and one of the leaders of the Irish, a man named Fenton, doffed his hat and passed it around. Similar events took place wherever Mitri said Mass or performed his priestly duties. His gratitude to the workers, most of all the Irish whom he had

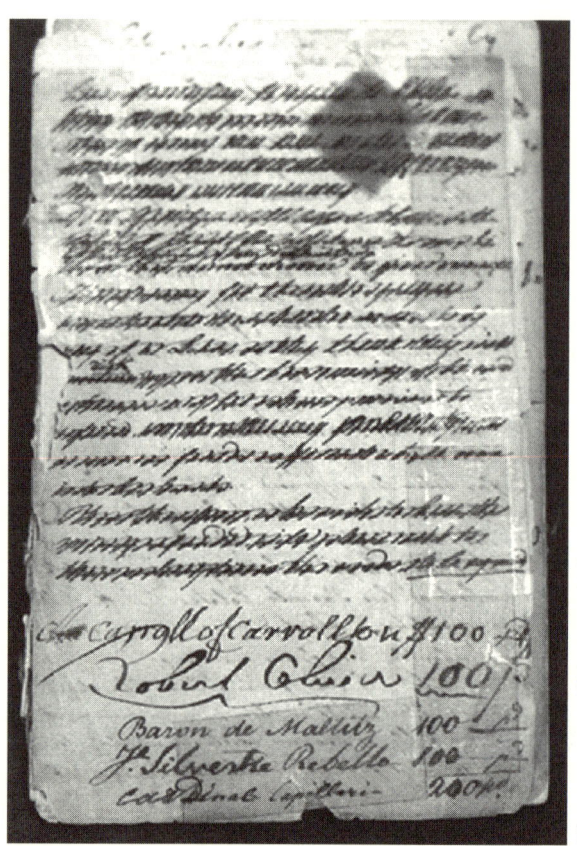

Fr. Gallitzin's receipt book. Note the entries for dontations from Charles Carroll of Carrolltown and Cardinal Cappellari, the future Pope Gregory XVI.

Photo courtesy of Mr. James Seiler

at times chastised for their drinking and wild ways, was clear in a letter to McCabe: "The noble Irish relieved me at once — they raised the money, and the urgent debt is paid."

The Protestants in the area proved a surprising source of funds. Protestant laborers contributed money to match the funds raised in the camps, and other Protestants proved eager to assist the now famous and immensely popular Catholic priest of the Alleghenies. The most remarkable display took place in the town of Blairsville as Mitri was on his way to a camp. When it was learned that he had arrived, local Protestant leaders held a rally for Mitri in the town hotel, heaping upon him praise for his work and his writings in defense of religious freedom and encouragement in the face of such troubles.

Through the deep sacrifices of the poor, both Protestants and Catholics, Mitri was able to save himself from his creditors and have the sale of his pastor's house canceled. Equally significant, his remaining creditors were so impressed with the events at Blairsville that they gave him extensions on the loans. Bolstered by the ardent support of his own people, Mitri at last was able to gain control over his financial situation. In succeeding years, all of his debts were paid off, easing the priest's mind and freeing up more money for his host of charitable programs.

Even as these events were unfolding, the Church in the United States was expanding rapidly. The central figure in this growth was Bishop Carroll, who headed the minority Church in a period of religious freedom that nevertheless was still troubled by pervasive anti-Catholicism. Laboring ceaselessly on behalf of the Church in America, Bishop Carroll increased both the number of priests in the country (from 24 in 1785 to 68 by 1808) and the Catholic population (from 25,000 in 1785 to about 100,000 by 1815).

By 1808 institutional expansion was possible with the proclamation from Rome elevating Carroll to the rank of Archbishop of Baltimore. This new structure brought with it four suffragan dioceses — Boston, New York, Philadelphia, and Bardstown, Kentucky. The latter city was chosen because of the sparkling success of missionaries in that region, most notably Father Charles Nerinckx, who had carried the famed gold watch from Europe for Mitri. The bishops consecrated for the dioceses were Jean Cheverus (Boston); Luke Concanen, O.P. (New York); Michael Egan, O.F.M. (Philadelphia); and Joseph Flaget, S.S. (Bardstown). Unfortunately, despite having created the new sees, the actual establishing of the dioceses by the newly named bishops was delayed by two years because of the situation in Europe.

Pope Pius VII (r. 1800-1823) refused to allow Napoleon to have his way with the Church in Europe, and the pope was seized in 1808. Though the pope was imprisoned and denied contact with his cardinals, if the French emperor hoped to break the spirit of Pius VII, he failed. The saintly pontiff returned to the monastic life of simple prayer that had been his way for many years as a simple Benedictine monk. Appointments remained unfilled as a result, and other administrative matters were left unattended or delayed. As for the American bishops, they could only be consecrated in 1810, and Bishops Cheverus and Egan were consecrated on October 28, 1810. (In 1813, Napoleon, facing enemy armies pressing down from all directions, finally released Pius VII as a gesture of goodwill to the Church.)

Mitri was invited to the consecration by Archbishop Carroll but declined. As usual, he did not have an assistant priest who could manage the affairs of the parish in his absence. There was also a reluctance to journey to Baltimore as it signaled the end of his time in service with Bishop Carroll as his leader. The new diocesan system meant that western Pennsylvania, including Loretto, fell under the jurisdiction of Bishop Egan of Philadelphia. His disappointment at losing his relationship with Bishop Carroll was expressed in a letter of congratulation to the archbishop in which he complimented him, "whose paternal affection, prudence and authority have so often afforded powerful protection against the poisonous shafts of slander and persecution."

Bishop Michael Egan, the bishop of Philadelphia and a member of the Franciscan Order, launched into his new post with considerable enthusiasm. The Irish-born prelate set out on a pastoral visit to Pittsburgh in 1811, and, naturally, he paid a call on the thriving parish in Loretto. While there, Egan confirmed 198 of Mitri's parishioners and presented a letter to the priest from his old friend and mentor, Father Brosius. In the letter, Brosius offered himself for the position of assistant pastor: "My desire is to be where you are, and to renounce the world which I do not love and which I have never loved. If I could be at all useful, I would consecrate the rest of my days willingly to you. . . ." There was the added incentive that Brosius' sister, who had recently married and had migrated to America, was desirous of moving to Loretto with her husband.

The pleasure of seeing his friend and adding to the community could not outweigh Mitri's grave concerns that Brosius was not up to the task of serving in the rugged regions of the Alleghenies, given his age and health. Bishop Egan concurred, and Mitri remained without an assistant. The bishop lamented to Archbishop Carroll the shortage of priests: ". . . without some timely aid from Europe, particularly from Ireland, I know not how to provide for the necessities of the diocese."

While the news from Europe was joyous — Pope Pius VII freed from his prison at Fontainebleau by Napoleon, for which Mitri offered a *Te Deum* sung in the chapel at Loretto — new political troubles started with the declaration of war between the United States and England in the War of 1812. It was a conflict in which Gallitzin played a small but memorable part and which demonstrated the priest's love and patriotic feelings for his new country.

America entered the war ill-prepared, and despite limited success on the seas, the fighting soon turned against America. An amphibious British force assailed the Chesapeake Bay area and captured Washington, D.C. Before withdrawing, the British set public buildings afire and caused national outrage. President Madison called for a day of prayer, and the order went out for all state militias to be organized.

Father Gallitzin joined in the day of prayer and shared the anguish over the burning of Washington. His sadness over the bloodshed was combined with the disappointment of America being at war with a nation that was serving as a leader in the struggle against Napoleon. Nevertheless, as a devoted American, Mitri supported his nation and volunteered his services.

Among the Pennsylvania regiments that were mustered for the war was the 142nd Pennsylvania Militia, comprised of parishioners from Loretto. Among the officers were several well-known Catholics, including Captain Richard McGuire, the son of old Michael McGuire, who wielded his father's Revolutionary War sword and Lieutenant John Feltz, Mitri's talented sacristan and cantor. Among the recruits was the giant John Weakland. Mitri wasted no time in offering to lend aid beyond his services as a chaplain.

Having been raised with military training, horsemanship, and fencing as part of his daily routine, Mitri was ideally suited to assist local woodsmen in preparing for war. Excellent hunters and trappers though they might have been, the Loretto militia was still in dire need of proper drilling and preparation for the dangerous and often confusing battlefields they were likely to encounter in the war. Fighting in the European model was very different from the free-wheeling and often very undisciplined tactics among the wilderness men.

McGuire and Feltz relied heavily upon Mitri in the training, learning from him the art of fencing, command in the field, and even how to vault over a horse, one of Mitri's favorites pastimes as a youth. Armed only with his walking stick, Mitri taught McGuire how to duel, disarming the younger and much bigger man with ease. The priest then stood as the region's unquestioned expert on drilling, giving powerful commands to the troops on how to march, present arms, fire in unison, fix bayonets, charge, and retreat in order. A nearby meadow served as a campground for the Loretto militia taking part in mock battles.

McGuire was finally satisfied that his troops were ready, and on the appointed day, he took his soldiers to St. Michael's Church, where they received Communion. After Mass, the regiment trooped its colors and soldiers, dressed in their homemade uniforms, and received, one by one, Father Gallitzin's blessing. As they marched away to a war Mitri regretted, he gave them a final blessing and told them, "Never forget you are a Buckskin."

McGuire's regiment did not arrive in the eastern battle area in time to participate in the repulse of the British at Baltimore. Instead, the unit was sent north to Niagara Falls to stand watch over the Canadian border. Stationed at Black Rock, New York, they gave support to the American attack on Canada at Niagara Falls, and participated in the taking of the Queenston Heights on the Canadian side. In the assault on the Heights, they were repulsed by the British when the New York militia failed to come to their aid.

After this brief participation in the fighting, the Loretto militia returned home to Pennsylvania in December, 1812, because the government could not find suitable winter quarters. Still, they could claim some measure of revenge for the burning of Washington. An even more crushing defeat of British troops came at the famed Battle of New Orleans which was actually fought after the war had ended. The Treaty of Ghent that resolved the conflict was signed on December 24, 1814, before the Battle of New Orleans on January 8, 1815; word did not arrive from Europe in time to prevent the waste of life.

Back in Loretto, Mitri continued to pray for the safety of the troops and to comfort the local parishioners as they worried about their husbands, fathers, and sons. On one occasion, a deserter from the Loretto regiment returned to the town and went straight to Father Gallitzin to explain his actions. The priest refused to take his hand, rebuking the soldier with the sharp words: "Leave my presence. I will not shake a coward's hand." Eventually, the other troops returned home, having spread the word of their pastor and drill master across much of the eastern United States.

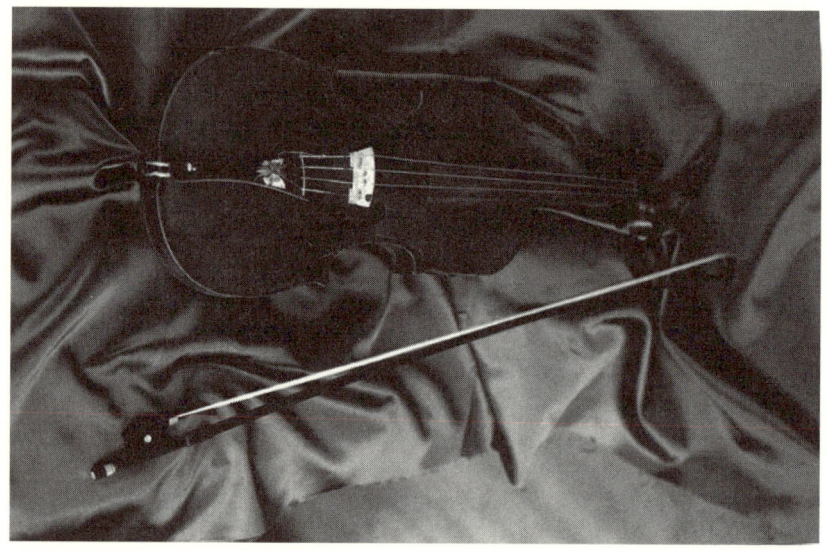

Fr. Gallitzin's violin. The instrument is still played. (Photo courtesy of Mr. James Seiler.)

Chapter Eight

Defense of the Faith

> *"As the days have gone by when it was possible for us to testify by martyrdom to God's glory upon earth, it becomes our duty, like the toil-worn ox, to remain hitched to the plow in the field of the Lord."*
>
> D. A. Gallitzin

The decades of faithful service at Loretto and the steady travails of journeys throughout the Alleghenies had truly transformed Mitri. His noble background and his profound sense of honor and duty had served as the foundation for his initial commitment. But the years at the altar, the hours in the confessional, his unstinting prayers and devotion in continuing had provided profound dimensions to his spiritual life. He had been molded by ministerial zeal and nearly consumed by his pastoral apostolate. He had also acquired considerable fame.

Mitri never sought publicity, but word of his remarkable dedication and perseverance spread across America. Such a reputation and acclaim did aid him with his parishioners. Because of his fame and esteem, his people relied upon him to act as a judge, and they were more inclined to follow his spiritual advice. But celebrity has both positive and negative aspects. For Mitri, the positive was the offer to elevate him to the episcopate as new dioceses were founded. The negative was displayed in attacks leveled against him and the Church.

Episodes of anti-Catholicism spurred Mitri into the role of one of America's early, gifted apologists. In this he followed in the footsteps of Charles Carroll of Carrollton, a signer of the Declaration of Independence and a fierce defender of the Catholic faith. Charles Carroll signed his works with the name "First Citizen." Mitri needed no protective shield when he wrote articles to deflect unwarranted and sometimes wholly unreasonable assaults by Protestants.

However, within his own ecclesiastical community Mitri was viewed with some uneasiness. One example of the somewhat equivocal judgments made about Mitri is visible in the events of 1814, when Bishop Egan of Philadelphia died after holding the post for less than four years. Mitri's name was considered immediately for the see, but his lifelong parochial assignment endangered such an appointment. Archbishop Carroll wrote strangely of his onetime priest:

> The Reverend Mr. Gallitzin has for many years lived so distantly that I cannot speak with confidence of his present dispositions. He has made sacrifices of worldly rank and performed actions of disinterested zeal; his literary and I presume theological requirements are considerable. But a strong objection to his preferment is a great load of debts, incurred rashly although for excellent and charitable purposes.

As it turned out, there were no immediate candidates deemed suitable, and the Philadelphia see remained vacant until 1820 when Irish-born Henry Conwell was named. By that time Mitri had made progress in the area of his debts, and other significant changes in the leadership of the Church in America had taken place. The most important development came on December 3, 1815, when Archbishop Carroll, architect of the Catholic faith in the United States, died at the age of eighty. He was succeeded in 1817 by Leonard Neale, who died after only two years, and then by the remarkable Ambrose Maréchal, S.S., whose service was desired both in the United States and Europe.

Owing to the size of his parish and his ever-growing celebrity status, Mitri was appointed vicar-general for western Pennsylvania by Bishop Conwell. This added to his reputation, and it was only natural that his was the first name mentioned when any new see became available. Among the dioceses that were offered to Mitri were Cincinnati and Detroit. The diocese of Cincinnati was created in 1821 as part of the division of the Bardstown diocese. Bishop Flaget wrote to Mitri asking if he would take over as the first bishop of Cincinnati. Mitri declined courteously. Years later, in 1833, when the diocese of Detroit was established, again Mitri was the favorite candidate. Speculation concerning the appointment was fueled by the gifted missionary priest Father Gabriel Richard, who had founded the University of Michigan and was the first priest in the U.S. House of Representatives.

This recommendation and the others that followed demonstrate Mitri's authenticity. The great missionaries and pastors of his era were able to evaluate him as his peers. They were on the frontlines of the faith, and they rated his decades of enduring pastoral labors with high regard as veterans of the same apostolate. Father Gabriel Richard genuinely hoped that Mitri would become the new bishop of Detroit. Before Richard died in 1832, he made up a will and left all of his earthly possessions to Father Gallitzin in the belief that Mitri could put them to good use as bishop. As expected, Archbishop Maréchal asked him to accept the new post. Once more Gallitzin declined.

He was committed to the people of the Alleghenies as his only flock and sought no other. His dedication centered on Loretto! There he had been called to serve, and there he would remain. While firm in his resolve, Mitri did take the opportunity to communicate with Archbishop Maréchal his hopes that a new diocese would be established in western Pennsylvania and that Loretto would be named the site of the see.

Mitri had been serving as a virtual vicar apostolic over the region for some time, given the still vast distances between Loretto and Philadelphia and the infrequent visitations by the bishop. The proposal thus seemed a logical one to him, echoing as it did the growing sentiment of a number of prelates, including Bishop Dubourg of New Orleans. The exact extent of the new diocese in western Pennsylvania was not certain, but the bishops were in agreement that Demetrius Gallitzin should be the first bishop. By this time, Mitri had paid most of his debts, and financial obligations were no longer a factor hindering his chances.

By 1829, the creation of a new diocese in western Pennsylvania was not high on the agenda of the bishops who gathered in Baltimore in October for the First Provincial Council of Baltimore. Rather, the first of seven provincial councils that would gather from 1829 to 1849 was concerned with organizing the Church in the United States and promulgating legislation that strengthened that organization. Thus, the assembled bishops and clergy decreed that, among other items, priests should remain in the dioceses to which they were assigned, careful and accurate registers of baptisms, marriages, confirmations, and burials should be maintained, Masses should be celebrated only in churches and stations approved by the bishop, and the odious custom of trusteeism should be abolished. The council, under the presidency of the newly appointed Archbishop James Whitfield (who received his pallium as metropolitan of Baltimore on October 4, 1829, the same day that the council opened), also took the step of electing, subject to the approval of Rome, a coadjutor bishop of Philadelphia to assure control of the diocese in the wake of Bishop Conwell's tragic tenure.

The aging Bishop Conwell, now eighty, had been buffeted since his consecration in 1820 by chronic difficulties with trustees, reach-

Several of Gallitzin's books, including his small personal spiritual diary. Also shown is his personal stamp with the family seal.

ing their most sad climax with the Hogan Schism, the dispute in Philadelphia involving Father William Hogan's split from the Church and the extreme actions of the trustees of St. Mary's parish. The gentle and exhausted Bishop Conwell finally resolved the schism in 1827, but his subsequent concessions to the trustees prompted a summons to Rome by Pope Leo XII and the appointment of an administrator in his absence. Upon his return, his official status was in question and authority remained with the administrator. To clarify matters, the American bishops petitioned the reinstatement of Conwell as bishop, but the council elected Francis Patrick Kenrick as coadjutor of Philadelphia in 1830, receiving the approbation of Rome. For the next twelve years, Kenrick was the effective administrator of the far-flung diocese. He ended the dominance of the trustees, founded the educational institute that became St. Charles Borromeo Seminary in 1833, and subsequently proved a capable and dedicated bishop.

Bishop Kenrick also displayed sensitivity to the priests under his jurisdiction. Aware that Father Gallitzin had been proposed for several sees — including the one in which Kenrick now served — he wrote to Mitri on May 3, 1830. Kenrick complimented Mitri for his many writing successes, urged him to remain as local vicar-general, and invited him to his consecration at Bardstown.

Mitri replied with a letter that expressed the priest's deep respect and affection for Bishop Conwell. As Mitri had faced his own trials with the trustees, he had only sympathy for the venerable bishop. Bishop Kenrick replied on June 11, 1830:

> ... Your letter exhibits the candid and uncompromising spirit of a missionary who, through a principle of duty, adheres to a prelate dear to his heart on account of obloquy and affections unjustly heaped upon him. I join fully with you in these strong and generous feelings, and I hope we shall both equally concur in the adoption of those measures which, in the judgment of the American prelates, and of the Holy See, seem necessary to terminate his afflictions. His age and his troubles demand, as they have thought, that he should be liberated from the burden of governing the diocese. ... A regard for his welfare, and a still greater concern for the interests of our holy religion in his diocese, induced my acquiescence when my youth, ill-health, and other circumstances, would have required my refusal of the episcopal dignity. God is my witness that I did not ambition it, and at this moment I could without a struggle part with the high but awful honor. ... Your piety and long-tried zeal promised me much aid in the arduous undertaking, and though the language of your answer would appear to me to be disheartening, I feel fully persuaded that on receiving

a distinct notification of my authority, you will support me most ardently in endeavoring to solace and honor the declining age of the venerable Bishop of Philadelphia, and to promote the peace and prosperity of the diocese. . . . The Bishop is still left at liberty to exercise all public functions, to administer confirmation, and even orders, to such as with my consent shall be presented for ordination. . . . Being solicited to go to Huntingdon by Rev. Mr. O' Reilly to dedicate a church and give confirmation, I may be prevented from calling on Loretto, which I greatly desire to do in order to form a personal acquaintance with its venerated pastor. If, in my power, I will gladly visit your congregation and administer confirmation at another time that may better suit. . . . Pray for me, dear Reverend Sir, and believe in the sincerity of my respect and attachment.

Francis Patrick Kenrick
Bp. Arath and Coadj. Phila.

    These letters signaled the start of a long relationship between Mitri and Bishop Kenrick. Once Father Gallitzin was informed fully of the actions of the Holy See and the American bishops, he embraced the new bishop with pious enthusiasm. The two men actually developed a deep spiritual association, and Bishop Kenrick visited Loretto six times between 1830 and 1835 for confirmations. This energetic bishop, whose diocese encompassed Pennsylvania, New Jersey, Delaware, and parts of New York, journeyed by horseback, rail, canal boat, wagon, and carriage across the rapidly developing but still frequently rugged countryside, making certain to stop at Loretto whenever possible to meet and confer with the prince-priest.

    The diary of Bishop Kenrick, written completely in Latin by the Rome-educated prelate, was translated and published in 1916. The work provides a number of interesting glimpses into life at Loretto in the 1830s. Kenrick wrote of his first trip to Loretto:

> October 30, 1830, we arrived at Ebensburg and on the 31st of the month I gave the Sacrament of Confirmation to more than a thousand persons at Loretto. The

Loretto congregation is very large and would require the strenuous efforts of three priests at least. The pastor, Reverend Demetrius A. Gallitzin, has reached an advanced age leading a life of the strictest integrity and labors that are marvelous. This remarkable man, while still quite young left the errors of the Greek (Schismatics), gave up his rights and dignities of a royal descent, and embraced the Catholic faith. There are two hundred acres of land adjoining the Church, a wooden building, the gift of a certain McGuire. The heirs of McGuire have not, however, as yet made out a deed which will secure the title to the property.

Five years, later he wrote:

Towards evening (July 9, 1835) I arrived at Loretto, the home of the Reverend Demetrius A. Gallitzin, who has lived here thirty-six years, and is in the sixty-fifth year of his life.

July the tenth day, I gave Confirmation to ninety-nine in the church of St. Michael's at Loretto.

The relationship between the bishop and Mitri was epitomized by the matters concerning the unfortunate priest, Reverend McGirr of Greensburg. In his first communication with Bishop Kenrick, Mitri asked the prelate not to undertake a hurried investigation into the rumored misconduct of McGirr whom Mitri, as vicar-general, had defended against what he considered to be vicious gossipmongers. Bishop Kenrick replied: "I did not intend to visit Rev. McGirr's congregation with the others on my way [to Pittsburgh], but I was determined not to adopt any precipitate measures. The information which you can afford me on this and other subjects will be most acceptable, and I hope to receive it by word or letter speedily."

After his stop at Loretto in October, 1830, Bishop Kenrick journeyed to Greensburg. There he looked into the charges and then made his decision. Reverend Mr. McGirr was transferred from Greensburg

Photo courtesy of the Prince Gallitzin Chapel House

The early Chapel House, built in 1832.

and sent to labor under Reverend Mr. Gallitzin as his assistant, replacing the newly ordained Reverend James Bradley who was to take up an assistant pastorship at Ebensburg. This compromise assignment to save the vocation of McGirr lasted only four years. Mitri was a model of patience with McGirr, but in the end, he could not prevent his fellow priest from falling back into bad habits. McGirr chose to leave Loretto, and Mitri wrote to Bishop Kenrick asking for a new assignment for the priest. Kenrick replied: "I do not think that I can give Reverend Mr. McGirr even a temporary appointment, as I have reason to believe that he does not honor his ministry.... The persons who surround him bring no credit to religion and his negligent habits are not calculated to gain respect for his ministry."

Bishop Kenrick remained Mitri's ordinary for the rest of the priest's life. The prelate's diary relates further visits to Loretto in 1838 and 1840, the latter taking place in the summer of 1840, after Mitri's death. The diary also records a reference to one of Mitri's illustrious relatives, Mother Elizabeth Gallitzin. Bishop Kenrick wrote:

> May 8, 1842. At the beginning of this month the nuns of the Most Sacred Heart of Jesus opened a convent in

McSherreytown, near Conewago. The lady Gallitzin founded this Convent; that is, Father Lekeu, S.J. transferred to her the house and lands formerly occupied by the Sisters of Charity.

Princess Elizabeth Gallitzin, Mitri's cousin, was born in 1797 in St. Petersburg to the Prince Alexis Andreievitch Gallitzin and the Countess Protasoff. Her mother was converted to Catholicism and several years later Elizabeth joined her. Subsequently, Elizabeth entered the Society of the Sacred Heart of Jesus at Metz, Lorraine, France, making her first profession in Paris in 1832. In 1834, she was appointed Secretary General of the congregation by the foundress, St. Madeline Sophie Barat. Named the visitatrix to the convents in the United States in 1840, she journeyed to the houses in Missouri and Louisiana, subsequently establishing convents in 1842 in New York City and in McSherreytown, in Pennsylvania, as noted by Bishop Kenrick. Mother Gallitzin also approved the opening of a mission among the Potowatomi Indians at Sugar Creek, Kansas and, during another visit in 1843-1844, labored with great heroism to alleviate the suffering caused by an outbreak of yellow fever. She herself succumbed to yellow fever at St. Michael's in Louisiana on December 8, 1843, surviving her cousin Mitri by fewer than three years.

As Bishop Kenrick noted in his first letter to Mitri, the priest had acquired a wide reputation as a writer and as an eloquent apologist for the Catholic faith. Mitri's talent was apparent even to Bishop Carroll, and it was as an apologist that the priest was able to apply all of his many skills and experience. Like other gifted Catholic writers who took up the pen to defend the faith, Mitri viewed his writings only as a stouthearted reply to anti-Catholic views being advanced by bigots. Mitri caused great consternation among his foes because of his rational, eloquent, and stinging rebukes, and he produced a host of conversions among his Protestant readers. The sensitivity, obvious goodness, and abundant conviction of the priest were revealed by his writings and earned him as well the respect and even admiration of both Catholics and Protestants throughout the United States and Europe. Thus, when Mitri visited Blairsville during one of his darkest hours — facing as he was financial ruin — the Protestants of that community gave him a warm welcome. They knew him as the beloved pastor of Loretto, but they were also familiar with him as a literary hero among American Catholics.

Mitri's debut in the literary scene began publicly in 1815-1816 with *Defence of Catholic Principles*, but Mitri had already provided a glimpse of his future talent as a writer back in 1808 when he responded to an attack made upon him in the political campaign of that year. After acquainting himself with his new country, Mitri had applied for citizenship in 1802, and he embraced his citizenship with utmost seriousness, following in Bishop Carroll's firm belief that Catholics in the United States had the obligation and the duty to be good citizens and to participate in all of the multifaceted aspects of life in the Republic. Through this participation, Catholics could demonstrate their rights to share in the full protection of the American constitution, to have a say in the functioning of the nation, to earn a place for themselves, and to curtail anti-Catholic propaganda that all Catholics were "foreign," hostile to democracy, and slaves in all things to the evils of "Romanism" and "Popery."

The desk used by Gallitzin in the Chapel House.

Photo courtesy of Mr. James Seiler

As was the privilege of all Catholics, Mitri could choose his own preference politically. He decided that the Federalist Party — the party of Washington and Madison — was the right one for him. While it was known that Mitri supported the Federalists, as the parish priest of Loretto he was always careful to remain neutral politically. He never sided openly with one candidate or another, at times to the consternation of his flock. In 1808, however, a political candidate sought to build his platform on Mitri's past.

In the contentious campaign of that year for the governorship of Pennsylvania, the Federalist candidate, an attorney from Pittsburgh named James Ross, faced a challenge from Simon Snyder, the son of German immigrants who had been a popular political leader, including a member of the House of Representatives from 1797-1808 and Speaker of the House for the last six years. One partisan, Charles Kenney, a lawyer from West Chester, near Philadelphia, sought to galvanize support for the nascent Republican Party (not the party that later formed in the 19th century) by sparking a controversy. He chose Mitri to be his flame.

Kenney had spent time in the McGuire's Settlement area and owned land in the Clearfields. He was familiar with life at the settlement and had even spent time in Mitri's own house. Putting this knowledge to malicious use, Kenney published a letter in *Dickson's Intelligencer* accusing Mitri of being a monarchist:

> The speculative opinions of Father Smith with respect to the different forms of government, are unfriendly to democracy. The pride of birth, early habits, and the prejudices of education may have operated on the mind of that gentleman to adopt Federalist principles, so congenial to his own, as Aristocracy and Federalism, or Monarchy, if you please are so closely assimilated.

Kenney's attack was based upon the increasingly known fact that Mitri was a European nobleman. The attack also used the claim that the Federalist Party favored such a strong central government that it harbored secret ambitions of establishing a monarchy.

Mitri published a reply to Kenney — who had adopted the *nom de plume* of Tyrconnel — on September 20, 1808, in the *Lancaster Gazette*. The article is an articulate defense of the priest's political principles and a point-by-point refutation of Kenney's charges against him and the Federalist candidate.

> The same religion [Catholicism] teaches me that the constituted authorities are the ministers of God serving unto his purpose: unto the purpose of guarding our political welfare, of protecting our persons, our property, our characters, [etc.] and that as such they ought to be respected and obeyed. The same religion

strongly inculcates the principle of loving and serving my Country, of cheerfully sacrificing my private interest to the support of that government which protects and shelters me, and of losing all I possess in this world rather than betray my Country. The same religion teaches me to respect in the highest degree the sanctity of an oath, and in particular of that oath by which I became a citizen of the United States, when in the most solemn manner I called upon the great God, the searcher of hearts, to witness my attachment and my future fidelity to the present Federal Constitution, and in particular to the Constitution of Pennsylvania. It teaches me that I am accountable to God for the use I shall make of those rights and privileges of citizenship secured to me by the Constitution, and it is with the greatest caution and under the influence of conscience, dictating upon as good information as can be procured, that I ought to give or refuse my vote. It teaches me that I am bound under the most sacred obligation (from which it would be criminal to depart) to vote into offices, those who are likely to be Political Shepherds, the fathers, the guardians, the protectors of their people, and to keep out the wolves in sheep's clothing who are willing to sacrifice the public welfare at the shrine of self-interest, those who wish to raise themselves on the ruin of the Constitution, so wise, so completely calculated to secure happiness to all who live under it — a Constitution which secures to all (without distinction) to the poor as well as the rich the unmolested enjoyment of the same privileges and liberties, a Constitution which respects the beggar's cottage as the President's palace, a Constitution that pries into man's conscience, but leaves it to each every one's choice to make the sign of the Cross or not to make it, to read the Bible in Latin or in English, to go to mass or a meeting, a Constitution which, even in the distribution of her offices, leaving the voice of the people, founded on the principle *vox populi, vox Dei* (the voice of the people, the voice of God) shows that she knows no distinction between man and man but that of merit and demerit. O happy Constitution! and happy those that live under her protection. Unhappy wretches those who in 1805 entrusted with legislative power and bound by oath to support the Constitution, at that time plotted her ruin and destruction! Shall we entrust power into the hands of such men again? Would we not, by so doing violate that sacred oath of fidelity by which we are bound to support the Constitution, and of course to keep out of office all those who testify their intention of using their influence for the purpose of destroying the Constitution?

Typical of Mitri's approach to opponents, within a few years he was once more on excellent terms with Kenney. This was proven by records dating to 1812. A deed shows that Mitri purchased sixty-four acres of land on the headwaters of Clearfield Creek. The owner of the land, called Hopewell, was Charles Kenney, Esq. James Ross lost to Simon Snyder, who went on to serve three terms as a popular governor.

Seven years later, another attack was made upon Mitri. This time the driving force was not politics, but anti-Catholicism. The response it drew was also far more vocal and ambitious, for Demetrius Gallitzin stood up and defended not merely his political principles as an American Catholic, but, the whole of the Catholic faith.

The controversy began in the early part of 1815 when the United States was still recovering from the War of 1812. At the darkest moment of the conflict, President Madison issued a proclamation asking for the recitation of public prayers to plead that Washington's capture be averted or, if unavoidable, that the harm arising from it be mitigated. The occasion of the prayer was used by a Protestant minister in Huntingdon, named Johnson, to deliver a vicious sermon against Catholics. Following the usual examples of anti-Catholic propaganda, Johnson's sermon proclaimed that the true enemies of America were Catholics; made evil by their superstitious habits, blind obedience to Rome, and heathen customs. Johnson assured his audience that Catholics could never make suitable citizens and were responsible for everything that was wrong, or could go wrong, in the United States.

The old St. Michael's and the Gallitzin Chapel House, 1891.

Word of the sermon eventually reached Mitri, and the priest wasted no time in replying. He sent his reply to the *Huntingdon Gazette* where it was published to a tumultuous public response. Given its success, Father Gallitzin was asked to enlarge the response which was then printed as a pamphlet and given wide circulation. The initial pamphlet was published in 1816 by the Pittsburgh printer, S. Engles, and subsequently, the work was translated into several languages, including French and German. It was read throughout the United States and found its way to Europe. Both in America and Europe, Gallitzin's place as one of Catholicism's leading apologists was assured, and the pamphlet was itself credited directly with bringing numerous converts into the Church.

Gallitzin's *A Defence of Catholic Principles in a Letter to a Protestant Minister* is a logical, clear, and well-organized examination of Catholic teachings that also reveal Mitri's long labors as a priest and his considerable knowledge about the doctrines of the faith. Throughout the *Defence* are dozens of footnotes and references to Scripture, apologetical and theological works (including Sts. Cyprian, Ambrose, John Chrysostom, Augustine, and Thomas Aquinas as well as the brilliant apologist Tertullian), and also Protestant writings by Luther, Forbes, and Cranmer. References were also made to conciliar documents of the Council of Trent, used not only to bolster his arguments but also to evidence the historical reality of the Catholic Reformation in the face of the challenge by Luther and Protestant Reformers.

Mitri had acquired much of his theological and catechetical knowledge during his days of study in Europe and especially in the seminary at St. Mary's, but this was supplemented and deepened by the years of solitude in the Alleghenies. He had arrived in the Clearfields area with a small library, adding to his collection with the generous assistance of his mother and other kind contributors. Before long, he could consult a library of six hundred volumes, spanning Catholic teachings, philosophy, theology, and spirituality, as well as works reflecting his wide-ranging intellect, including a volume, in Dutch, on navigation. Most of his books were in French and Latin, others were in English, Italian, or German. Among his favorite works were those by St. Aquinas, St. Teresa of Ávila, St. Augustine, Bossuet, Fenelon, and Massillon. Of particular interest — given the worn appearance of the volumes after his death — were Bourdaloue's *Retraite Spirituelle* (*Spiritual Retreat*, Paris, 1747) and Abbé Lamourette's *Devotion au Sacre Coeur de Jesus* (*Devotion to the Sacred Heart of Jesus*, Paris, 1785). Noticeably absent from his library were the books on current philosophy, such as Goethe, Voltaire, Rousseau, and Locke, volumes that were expected in any self-proclaimed intellectual's collection. Mitri had grown up in such a philosophical arena and had rejected it. There was no need for these books — Mitri understood their errors and their detrimental effects.

The literary works did not sit unread on the shelves. Mitri pored over them voraciously when he was alone. As his later assistant, Father Lemcke, wrote: "Whenever Father Gallitzin went, he always carried a book of theological or ascetical content in his pocket. St. Thomas (Aquinas) or a volume on Church history was always on the table." He was thus ideally prepared to confront Reverend Johnson with the Protestant's own weapons: Scripture, history, and the writings of the Reformers.

The *Defence* begins with a Preface that makes evident his reasons for writing the apology:

> A SERMON preached by a Protestant minister on a day appointed by the government for humiliation and prayer in order to avert from our beloved country the calamity of war, has been the occasion of the present letter.
>
> The professed subject of his sermon on such a day was, or should have been to excite his hearers to hu-

mility and contrition, and to a perfect union of hearts and exertions during the impending storm. But he, very likely alarmed at a much greater danger of which no one else but himself dreamed; alarmed, I mean, and trembling for the ark of Israel likely to be carried off by those Philistines called Roman Catholics; or alarmed perhaps at the very real danger of an intended invasion from the Pope who would, be sure, avail himself of the confused state of the country to assist his English friends in the conquest of it that he might by means extend his jurisdiction; or in fine, alarmed lest our treacherous Catholics would take advantage of the times and, by forming a new Gunpowder Plot, would blow up the Congress hall, Senate houses and all the Protestant meeting house of the United States; alarmed at least by something or another, he suddenly forgets his subject and, putting on a grave countenance, enters into the most solemn caveat against Popish and Heathen neighbors, cautioning his hearers against their superstitions, and gives them plainly enough to understand that such Popish neighbors are not to be considered their fellow citizens.

Attacks of that kind being so common in this liberal country, I have always treated them with silent contempt. The present one proceeding from a respected quarter I thought necessary to notice; and I expected a few respectful lines which I published in a Gazette would have been sufficient to draw from the gentleman an apology for his uncharitable expressions. I found myself deceived in my expectation. After having waited in vain from September until some time in the winter I made up my mind to send to the gentleman the following DEFENCE OF CATHOLIC PRINCIPLES.

Gallitzin then offers a "Summary of the Catholic Doctrine," followed by specific explanations of sacraments ("Confession," "The Eucharist or Lord's Supper," "The Sacrifice of the Mass," "Communion under One Kind or Form"), and other teachings ("Purgatory and Prayers for the Dead," "Honouring the Saints and applying their Intercession," "Images, Pictures, and Relics," "The Pope," and "Toleration"). In his "Conclusion" Mitri writes:

> For God's sake, dear sir, if you value the glory of God and the salvation of your soul, give up protesting against the Catholic Church. In it alone you will find salvation. As sure as God lives, it is the true Church of Christ. May the day of judgment be for me the day of God's total vengeance if the holy Roman Catholic Church is not the only one, true and immaculate spouse of Christ. May my soul be doomed to suffer for you to all eternity all those torments which you would deserve by following the superstitions of the church of Rome.
>
> Hush into silence your prejudices; listen and adore; humble yourself with St. Paul into the very dust, pray for light, and you shall see it brighter than the dazzling rays of the mid-day sun. Ask for grace to overcome human respect and all carnal considerations, those obstacles which Satan raises to prevent the conversion of millions, and that grace will be imparted to you. Seek the kingdom of heaven by which in scripture language is often meant the church of Christ, the Catholic Church, as yet in a state of suffering, persecuted, ridiculed, tried like gold in the furnace, as yet wandering through the dreary and frightful desert, but on its way to the land of promise; you will find it, and with it you will enter the mansions of eternal peace. That you and all your hearers may obtain the blessing of blessings is the sincere desire and shall be the constant prayer of
> Your humble and obedient servant,
Demetrius A. Gallitzin

It took two years for Reverend Mr. Johnson to publish his reply to the *Defence*, in the form of a small book, *Vindication of the Doctrines of the Reformation.* The polemic made no effort to refute Mitri's personal concerns, nor did it concern itself with the many points of Catholic doctrine and the Reformation. When asked about this rather obvious omission, Johnson would say only that the *Defence* "was too despicable to merit reply." Instead, Johnson unleashed even greater anti-Catholic fury, railing against Catholics and their practices without restraint or even attempt at courtesy.

The *Vindication* brought a renewal of the storm of controversy, and both Catholics and Protestants awaited eagerly Mitri's answer. The priest understandably found Johnson's *Vindication* too vicious to warrant — or even need — a direct reply. Instead, he penned "An Appeal to the Protestant Public," printed in 1819 at Ebensburg. This was followed by the more directed answer to *Vindication* in the form of *A Letter to a Protestant Friend on the Holy Scriptures (Being a Continuation of the "Defence of Catholic Principles"),* printed in 1820 in Ebensburg.

The *Appeal* and *Letter* differed from the *Defence* in several ways. First, they are more casual and generally accessible in their tone and style. While strong in their academic level —more so the *Letter* — there are none of the footnotes that are sprinkled throughout the *Defence.* Further, the writings are more focused, refuting the claims of Reverend Mr. Johnson and examining in more detail the Holy Scriptures. The *Letter* is divided into "The Canon of Scripture," "The True and Faithful Translation of Scripture," "The True Sense of Scripture," "Some Other Matters" ("The Celibacy or Single Life of the Clergy," "The Holy Office of the Inquisition," "Works of Supererogation," "Persecution of Protestants," "Miracle Wrought by the Priests and Monks," and "The Mass Celebrated in an Unknown Tongue"), "A Suggested Letter for the Protestant Minister," and a "Postscript."

Mitri writes in the *Letter:*

> In the Letter to a Protestant Friend, I give to the public at the request of some respectable friends, who are of the opinion that it may be of benefit to other Protestants besides the one to whom it is directed. In my "Appeal to the Protestant Public," I have stated my reasons for not addressing the Protestant minister any more. His ungentlemanly language, together with the many falsehoods he advances in order to expose the

Catholic cause to the hatred and contempt of the public, plainly shew that he is not actuated by motives of charity, and that he is blinded by passion; of course, not open to conviction. However, truth compels me that I am, nevertheless, indebted to him for affording me a considerable degree of assistance in converting Protestants to the Catholic faith. His "Vindication of the Doctrines of the Reformation," gave the finishing stroke to several of them, who after reading Catholic principles in Catholic books, were very curious to know what arguments Protestant writers could have to oppose those principles. They read the "Vindication" with great attention, and read it again: what was the result? They came to me, and prayed to be admitted members of the Catholic Church. On the first Sunday of October (after having made their sacramental confession) six of them made their public profession of faith, before the altar at St. Michael's church of Loretto, according to the rites and ceremonies prescribed by the Roman ritual, renouncing their errors, and promising before God and the congregation, to live and die in the Roman Catholic Church. Since that time several more Protestants have applied to me, and testified an eager desire to become members of the holy Catholic Church of Christ. If I had any favor to ask of the Protestant minister, it would be that he continue to write against the Catholic church, and to vindicate the doctrines of the Reformation.

Concerning Scripture, Mitri cleverly writes in the *Appeal:*

> I freely confess, my dear brethren, that I am no match for the Protestant Minister; for he hath the Holy Scripture at his command, can squeeze into any shape, or make it say what he pleases; he therefore can never be at a loss. I on the contrary, am so convinced of my ignorance, of my inability to interpret Scripture, that in all cases, confine myself to the interpretation which

the Holy Catholic Church gives me: because my Savior Christ has promised, that the Spirit of Truth shall remain with the Apostles forever, John XIV. 16, 17.

He adds in the *Letter:*

> We respect the Bible at least as much as you do. We believe it to be divinely inspired. We read it with fear and trembling. We kiss the sacred text every time we read the gospel of the day, in the Mass. But we do not presume to interpret it: we do not throw precious pearls before the swine. We caution our hearers against the danger of self interpretation; and do publicly acknowledge that we are not able, by the utmost exertion of our mental powers, to fathom its profound mysteries. We do preach from scripture, it is true; but far from presuming to put our own interpretation on the sacred text we deliver our to hearers that interpretation which the Catholic Church gives us, believing the Church to be guided by the spirit of truth forever, (John XIV. 16), believing Christ the fountain of truth and the salvation to be with his ministers until the consummation of the world (Mat. XXVIII. 20). . . . Thus all our interpretations of all essential parts of scripture, are exactly alike; and were you to listen to a Catholic minister in Pekin [modern Beijing] in China, or at Loretto in Cambria county, Pennsylvania, you would find everywhere the same interpretation, the very same doctrine.

Of additional value to many of his readers were Gallitzin's defense of celibacy, persecution of Protestants, and the Mass in Latin. All three were particular targets of abuse by anti-Catholics. Of celibacy, Mitri wrote a specific and historical anecdote:

> Some years ago, when that dreadful contagion raged against the prisoners of war confined in the king's house, London, which carried off so many hundreds, numbers of them, who were French Protestants, called

upon Protestant ministers for that attendance which they saw administered to the Catholic prisoners by one or two priests. They called in vain; which caused those Protestants prisoners to apply to the priests to die Catholics. What was the excuse of the Protestant ministers for not attending? It was what might be expected: "We are not more afraid," said they, "as individuals, to face death in the discharge of our professional duties, than the priests are, but we must not carry a poisonous contagion into the bosom of our families."

As for the persecution of Protestants, Mitri was vehement in assuring his readers:

> The Catholic Church so much abhors persecution for the sake of religion, that the clergymen of that church have upon all occasions exerted their zeal to prevent it and to oppose it . . . and the Catholic Church so much abhors the shedding of blood, or any acts of cruelty, that by a law of said church, all those are excluded from ordination, and, are declared irregular who either directly or indirectly have any hand in the effusion of blood, even although no crime is thereby committed. . . .

Finally, Mitri uses four points to defend the celebration of the Mass in Latin: Latin is a dead language, not subject to the changes that characterize living tongues and thereby impacting upon Catholic liturgy; Latin "establishes a uniformity in the service throughout the whole world"; despite priests hailing from many countries, the Latin Mass permits any priest to celebrate the Eucharist anywhere in the world; lastly given the presence in the Mass of "tremendous mysteries" the sacred words contained within it "ought not be exposed to profanation, therefore they are pronounced in a language only known to the more improved classes of society."

Mitri concludes the initial *Letter* (he appended a postscript):

> My dear friend, if the above advice appears to you rational and comfortable to what you already know of

the word of God, you will take it. After meditating seriously on the subject, you will let me know your sentiments; and you may expect to hear more on the subject, from

> Your humble servant, And friend,
> Demetrius Gallitzin
> March 29, 1819

Much as the *Vindication* was itself sufficient to deter intolerance, Mitri was also hopeful of promoting conversions by the more positive influence of his writings. At the very least, he prayed that his Protestant readers might appreciate more fully the Catholic Church and respect as they should the rights of Catholics everywhere. This hope is threaded throughout the *Defence* and in both the *Appeal* and *Letter*. He must have been delighted with the result when Protestant readers, traveling through Loretto or journeying deliberately to meet him, arrived to pay their respects and to give him encouragement. There were many others who came to Mitri with the sole intention of becoming Catholic.

As a convert to the faith, and as one raised in an environment hostile to all religion, especially Christianity, Mitri was able to express and validate the emotions and longing of the catechumens who came to him for advice and instruction. At the heart of his teaching was his unshakable faith in the Church.

> Do not be deceived; there is only ONE LORD, ONE FAITH, AND ONE BAPTISM. (Eph. IV.) Only ONE Church, raised by the hands of Jesus Christ, against which all powers of hell shall never prevail. (Mat. XVI. 18.) Only ONE church in which the Spirit of Truth abides for ever.... Search for the scriptures; they clearly point out to you the Church as our only guide in the way of salvation. It is to her, and not their own dead letters, they send you for instruction....

As the years passed after the publication of his works, Mitri's fame continued to increase. His writings circulated throughout Europe and new editions were in constant production, with one of the most notable editions of the *Defence of Catholic Principles* published in 1821. He also served as an example for any drawn to the Catholic faith. With his single-minded dedication, however, Mitri remained the pastor of Loretto, undertaking any and all tasks to benefit the community. To aid in his apostolate of conversion, he took out an advertisement in March 22, 1825, in the *Cambria County Gazette:*

> Notice
> A certain number of Protestants have manifested a great desire in becoming members of the Roman Catholic Church. I hereby acquaint the said Protestants and the public in general that I have appointed the Second Sunday after Easter (17 April) for admitting them into the Church, according to the Rites and Ceremonies of the Roman Ritual.
>
> Demetrius Gallitzin
> Parish Priest

And yet, anti-Catholicism remained a real part of life in America, and Mitri was vigilant in opposing it. Thus, early in 1834, he authored a series of six letters in reply to a gathering of Presbyterian parsons in Columbia, Pennsylvania. These ministers resolved to publish Presbyterian tracts and books "inculcating the distinctive doctrines of our standards, etc." The resolution added various levels of anti-Catholicism and drew Mitri's fire in an elaborate response.

Collectively known as *Six Letters of Advice to the Gentlemen Presbyterian Parsons (Who Lately Met at Columbia, Pa. For the Purpose of Declaring War Against the Roman Catholic Church),* the individual letters were first published in newspapers and then in pamphlet form, including an edition by Canan and Scott, in Ebensburg, in 1834. In the very first letter, Gallitzin begins with humor:

> Well done, gentlemen! Thus, you have sounded the tocsin of war. You have drawn the sword and thrown away the scabbard. Like so many heroes you stand in battle array to fight the battles of the Lord against Pope and Popery. Fame, which hath already wafted across the

Atlantic the account of deeds during the ravages of the cholera [when the ministers refused to minister to the dying], will bring your declaration of war to Rome, and will fill it with terror and dismay.

But now, gentlemen, let me tell you it is not sufficient to know how to declare war; you ought also know how to carry it on; and I am somewhat acquainted with military tactics (having formerly held a commission in the Russian army), charity compels me to assist you with advice.

With remarkably modern imagery, Mitri notes in his second letter:

After having spent some hours in your laboratory, in making up a monster composed of idolatry, superstition, cruelty, etc., etc., hideous enough to frighten the devil out of his kingdom, you are to mount the pulpit, and there exhibiting the monster, the work of your own creation, you are to work yourselves into a holy rage, call the monster Genuine Popery, and consign it and use the lowest pit.

He then gently but emphatically points out the ludicrousness of their position, challenging them to prove that they "are true ministers of Christ, not impostors...."In the fourth letter he suggests:

Gentlemen Parsons, if you are to succeed in your undertaking of pulling down what you call Romanism, you will have to devise new means; for all those who have tried, since the pretend reformation, have proved vain and fruitless.... Now, tell me, gentlemen, do you really think that if you could ever persuade the people of the United States to alter the Constitution, so as to deprive the Catholics of their citizenship, and by laws enacted for that purpose, have them reduced to beggary, and subjected to the punishment of death, for hearing Mass or for going to confession, do you think that you would then get your ends accomplished? Oh no!

He concludes with a final, biting suggestion:

> Conceal from your hearers the fact that, in the East Indies Mission alone, the Catholic missionaries are (as we are told by the London papers) to your Protestant missionaries as three hundred to one! Above all things, don't let them know that the Pages of the Bible which you send by millions to all parts of the globe, are (as we are told by a letter from the British Lieutenant Slade, a Protestant) by many of them used as a wadding for their guns. Conceal all these things from your hearers, for fear that, growing cool in the work of charity, of throwing pearls before swine, the rivers of dollars would shrink into small rivulets, and perhaps finally dry up altogether.

The last of Mitri's famed works was again concerned with Scripture, a topic regularly used by anti-Catholics to assail the Church. In this case, Mitri was responding in the middle 1830s to the then widely read religious periodicals that spread anti-Catholic propaganda. The main cause of the tract, *The Bible: Truth and Charity* was a work in the *Christian Herald* (No. 20, Vol. 7), published by a minister in Pittsburgh, and filled with the usual paranoia and predictable tirades against Popery, Rome, and Catholic priests.

Referring to the author as "Gentlemen?" Mitri prefers to make light of their laughable attacks and to focus instead on the biblical passages pertaining to truth and charity. Demonstrating a sweeping command of Scriptures, he quotes some fifty separate passages on the Catholic embrace of truth and charity, asking his Protestant readers:

> That Charity, if genuine, embraces the whole human race, not excluding any individuals, on the score of differences either in political or religious opinion. By what kind of logic, then, will you attempt to prove that by far the greater number of Christians — I mean the Roman Catholics — may be excluded from your Charity, and may lawfully be considered as objects of your hatred, spite, and malice?

As for the propaganda:

> I must candidly confess, Gentlemen? that I have never, in all the days of my life, met with such a charivari of malicious nonsense. Any attempt, therefore, on my part, to confute the above assertions, might appear as trifling, as so much time wasted, were it not well known that the most palpable falsehoods, when proceeding from a respectable quarter, are received as Gospel by the multitude.

Writing in the full maturity of his priestly life, Mitri summons up a host of innovative and convincing points, routing the claims of the article in the *Christian Herald*. Mitri quotes the Roman writer Livy, Luther, and assorted Protestant authors. He finishes with eloquence as a Catholic, and an American:

> Whatever differences on points of doctrine may exist amongst the different denominations of Christians, all should be united in the bonds of Charity, all should pray for another, all should be willing to assist one another; and, where we are compelled to disapprove of our neighbor's doctrine, let our disapprobation fall upon his doctrine only, not upon his person.
>
> Thus the sacred cause of religion will be effectually promoted and thus the Commonwealth will be safe. United we stand; divided we fall.

Chapter Nine

The Twilight Era

> "Our age, dear sir, is the age of incredulity commonly called the age of philosophy. It is almost fashionable to disbelieve, to reject with disdain and contempt everything which we cannot perceive with our carnal senses, compass with our limited and much corrupted understanding. At the hour of death at the entrance of eternity when the senses shall have lost their baneful influence and corrupted reason shall be almost extinguished, we shall remember that there is an omnipotent God who can do what He pleases...."
>
> D.A. Gallitzin

From the time of his arrival at McGuire's Settlement in 1799 until 1829 when Father Patrick Rafferty was named his first formal assistant, Demetrius Gallitzin had served virtually alone as pastor of Loretto and chief missionary of the Alleghenies. To remain with his beloved parishioners, Mitri declined numerous offers of elevation to the episcopacy and instead devoted himself entirely to his people in the truly Catholic community that he had founded. Through his personal labors and ceaseless missionary undertakings, Mitri was solely responsible for the creation of missions at Bedford, Ebensburg, Frankstown, Hart's Sleeping Place, Newry, Huntingdon, Jefferson (Wilmore), Johnstown, Sinking Valley, Summit, and Somerset. By 1839, what had been originally the small Catholic community of McGuire's Settlement had grown to 5,000 Catholic families in Cambria County, a fact that was a source of joy to Mitri always.

Just as the Catholic community had grown and developed, so too had the landscape of western Pennsylvania. Cities and towns were emerging out of the wilderness, and the once rough-hewn trails were being replaced by roads. Paved thoroughfares, however, were not the permanent solution that Pennsylvania needed to connect Philadelphia with the western region of the Commonwealth, especially Pittsburgh. The mountains were too forbidding and the weather too severe in the Alleghenies for roads to be sufficient methods for developing the state. The success of the Union Canal made possible more ambitious projects, including the hope of creating a through-state canal. Such a grand scheme was prevented only by the Alleghenies, for the ridges represented a thirty-six mile wall between the water routes of the Juniata and the Conemaugh. The solution was to build a railroad to transport the passengers and boats over the mountains from the Juniata Division at Hollidaysburg to the Western Division at Johnstown. The result was the Allegheny Portage Railroad, opening in 1834.

The immense achievement of the Allegheny Portage Railroad also signaled the end of the grand canal system. To the north of the Portage Railroad, the Pennsylvania Railroad defeated the mountains in a spectacular way with the Horseshoe Curve, situated along an old Indian path to Kittanning, the very path used by Mitri as he made his way to McGuire's Settlement. Life in Pennsylvania would never be the same again, and Mitri watched all these developments from his parsonage at Loretto.

He saw the work on the canals and railroads as instruments of serious pastoral obligations. These public projects had attracted thousands of laborers, and most of them were Catholics. The Irish, Germans, and other Catholics often went for weeks, even months, without a priest or the sacraments. Mitri cared for them as best he could, visiting their grim and squalid camps to celebrate Mass and hear confessions. He also took his violin with him to serenade the camp and offer moments of solace. The workers, in turn, honored the priest by giving timely and desperately needed aid during his financial difficulties.

Even as Pennsylvania matured around him and the population grew, Mitri never wavered from his commitment to Loretto. Despite the presence of assistants, he carried the main load of work as the pastor of several generations of Catholics. The children he had baptized were now married, the orphans he had raised were now adults, and he had buried many of the very souls he had welcomed to the mountain.

As a new added symbol of the permanence of life at Loretto, in 1832 Mitri added an adjoining chapel to his already expanded house.

Named St. Mary's Chapel, this small house of worship permitted the aging priest to celebrate Mass in comfort in the bitter days of winter, instead of in his unheated church. The chapel boasted several innovations as well, reflecting Mitri's awareness of progress.

He ordered the carpenter to cut a special window from the chapel to the upper level that afforded a view of the Blessed Sacrament from the second floor. He also raised a trestle outside. There he hung a bell instead of using a bell tower. The bell was of foreign make and had such a distinctive ring that it was dubbed by its hearers across the valley as the "Russian Bell." The altar candlesticks were carved from curly maple. Mitri spent long hours in prayer in the chapel, especially as his health started to decline as the result of his years of labor.

The house that had begun as a simple log cabin with a kitchen was now large enough to aid Mitri in his care of orphans. In fact, he took for himself only two small rooms on the left side of the house. The remainder was for his housekeeper and the orphans.

His daily routine was one given over entirely to service, taken up by the sacraments, physical labor, and traveling to the far-flung missions under his care. He was up before dawn and spent each day riding across the rugged mountains in the heat of summer or in the shattering cold of winter. The distances demanded the use of horse, and Mitri, of course, was a superb equestrian. When visiting a distant community, he would normally spend the evening with one of the families, rising very early the next morning and preparing the altar (thus converting a simple home into what was commonly called a "Mass House"). Prior to the Mass, Mitri would hear confessions and then make certain that the small Catholic congregation was prepared for the sacrament. After Mass, Mitri would give advice and additional instructions to his hosts and would normally take extra care and time to provide catechetical teaching to any children present. This was often the only instruction the children might receive, and the brief classes had to be memorable. Only after all his tasks were completed did Mitri finally take food, a meal that as many times as not came late and often did not sit well with his sensitive stomach. If he remained in Loretto, he spent his time serving as a confessor, priest, counselor, judge, and when necessary, as an arbitrator between quarreling parties.

Such an apostolic regimen was hard and took its toll. As biographer Daniel Sargent wrote: "Mitri was sixty-five and he looked eighty-

The Gallitzin window in St. Joseph's Church. (Photo courtesy of Fr. Tim Stein, *The Catholic Register*.)

five." Described as elegant, slender, and always prone to an upset stomach or minor intestinal ailment, Rev. Dr. Gallitzin, as he was called by his people, endured with signs of grace becoming more and more evident. Disease was a constant threat on the frontier, with cholera, yellow fever, and typhoid taking many lives, and while Mitri avoided these, a minor infection caused him permanent injury — he allowed himself to be treated by one of the dubious medical practitioners who flourished in the wilds of America. Mitri watched as his teeth fell out, a side effect of the mysterious elixir the charlatan doctor provided. Mitri's assistant pastor, Reverend James Bradley, recalled seeing the bright white teeth sitting in a desk drawer. Gallitzin observed cheerfully, "There they are, perfect, but I cannot use them."

By 1829, Mitri was approaching his sixtieth year, and there was some thought that a permanent assistant could be of help in easing his burden. Reverend Patrick Rafferty was dispatched from Philadelphia and took up the post as assistant pastor. Rather than serve at Loretto, Father Rafferty was sent by Mitri to Ebensburg. Here he remained for the duration of his service in the area. After Rafferty came Father Bradley, and then a priest who earned a special place in the life of Mitri, Reverend Peter Lemcke.

Both as pastor and vicar-general for that part of Pennsylvania, Mitri found support and friendship from other priests in the region. Two of the more notable neighboring priests were Reverend James A. Stillinger and Reverend Thomas Heyden. Like Lemcke, both priests had close dealings with Reverend Gallitzin and left vivid pictures of the pastor of Loretto and his life in the mountains.

Father Stillinger was sent to Loretto soon after his ordination. The new priest was the grandson of James Stillinger, the Catholic farmer who had saved Father Brosius from a gang of Protestant assassins years before and had been visited by Mitri back in the 1790s. Reverend Stillinger thus had an immediate connection to Mitri, one that was deepened further when Stillinger took up his post as pastor at Blairsville, a new church situated on the site of the original Irish camp. Stillinger wrote of their meeting:

> In 1831 I went to see Father Gallitzin for the first time. On entering the hall he met me, and took my hand with both of his, so beautifully framed. He looked into my face with his dark hazel eyes, quick and penetrating. His countenance beamed with benevolence and kindness. His address was graceful, bland, fatherly and accomplished, as at once to indicate the nobleman and the self-sacrificing convert and missionary. Before I could give my address, he said: "Your name is Stillinger; I said Mass in your grandfather's home before you were born. You are welcome."

Over the next year, Stillinger grew in his admiration for the older pastor, but even his high praise paled in comparison to the boundless loyalty paid to Mitri by the Reverend Thomas Heyden. Born in 1793 in County Carlow, Ireland, he had been brought to America as an infant. His father settled in Bedford and opened a store for trade that was ideally situated along the main highway leading from Philadelphia. Thomas Heyden had grown up with Father Gallitzin as a regular element in his life, for the priest regularly visited his family, spent the night, and traded in his father's store. Throughout his youth, Heyden had received encouragement for his vocation, and to the great delight of Mitri, entered St. Mary's Seminary. Ordained on May 21, 1821, he was sent to Loretto to receive guidance from Gallitzin as to where his energies could best be directed. The pastor sent him to the southeast of Loretto, around Bedford, including the mission stations of New Baltimore, Hollidaysburg, Sinking Valley, Huntingdon, and Shade Gap. He also became associated closely with the church at Newry.

The little stone church at Newry had been built in 1816, and was dedicated by Mitri under the patronage of St. Patrick. It therefore lays claim to Mitri as its first pastor — Heyden was its second — and the honored position of being the second church in the region established by Gallitzin. Father Heyden assumed duties as visiting pastor in 1821, remaining so until 1831, when Reverend John O' Reilly was appointed by Bishop Kenrick as resident pastor. Subsequently, Heyden held a variety of posts in the see of Natchez, Mississippi. He declined elevation to the episcopacy, perhaps in emulation of Mitri (who had been such an influence on him), and stayed as pastor in Bedford until his death in 1870. Heyden held a special place in the life of Mitri not only for being a protégé but for authoring a life of the Loretto missionary. First published in 1869, *A Memoir on the Life and Character of the Rev. Prince Demetrius A. de Gallitzin* was written for a specific reason:

> The Author of this sketch who, for almost a quarter of a century, had been bound by the closest bonds of amity with the Reverend Prince, has been frequently urged by respected friends, to compose and publish a notice of his life. . . . The writer could not resist any longer the many appeals made to him to give to the public all the reminiscences he had of his lamented friend. . . . Moreover, he became alarmed, lest many traits of his life would quickly be forgotten and perish, if not at once secured and perpetuated by the press. If this labor of love was not attended to presently, it was said the few remaining contemporaries of the Reverend Prince Gallitzin would soon sink into the tomb, and thus much of important material would be lost forever.

Written when Father Heyden was quite late in life, the biography is an earnest, even reverential, account that reflects the author's abiding fondness and regard for Mitri. While far from a critical biography in the traditional sense of historical writing, Father Heyden's work does include numerous letters, a rare autobiography by Gallitzin, and details on the events following Mitri's passing. Above all, the book is a testament to the degree to which Mitri left his spirit and prayerful influence upon virtually everyone who worked with him or came to know him.

Father Heyden was not alone in his desire to leave a written record of his years with Mitri. Another priest, Reverend Peter Henry Lemcke, assisted Mitri for six years, from 1834-1840, and was his direct successor as pastor at Loretto. For these reasons, along with Lemcke's biography of the priest and his genuinely special place as a friend and support to Mitri in his last years, Lemcke has earned a unique honor in Catholic American history.

Born in Mecklenburg, Germany, in 1796, Lemcke grew up in a generally unhappy family, and his parents devoted little energy to his education. A bright and studious young man, Lemcke was able to receive a decent education thanks to his grandfather and a local doctor, but his home life was so unpleasant that he ran away twice. The second time he journeyed to Schwerin, where he began a formal education. After a number of years as a soldier in the Prussian army during the terrible Napoleonic Wars, he embarked on studies to become a Lutheran minister at the University of Rostock. He graduated in 1819, but his career as a Lutheran minister proved short-lived. Dissatisfied with his life and much influenced by the example of his Catholic friends, Lemcke was converted and received into the Catholic Church in 1824. In just two short years, he was ordained a Benedictine priest (later he entered the Benedictines), and he spent several more years working in the diocese of Ratisbon. Then, one day, a friend showed him a letter from Bishop Kenrick in which the bishop of Philadelphia appealed for more priests from Europe. Hearing the call, Father Lemcke resolved to devote himself forever to the Church in the New World. In 1834, he arrived in the United States and was assigned briefly at Holy Trinity Church, Philadelphia. Bishop Kenrick soon reassigned him to the Alleghenies, with the task of serving as assistant pastor to the legendary Prince Demetrius Gallitzin.

Father Lemcke had heard often in Europe about the exploits of Mitri, and, indeed, the missionary had been an inspiration to him in his decision to give his life to the Church in America. Mitri's writings and reputation as a selfless missionary in the wilderness had not been forgotten, nor had Countess Amalia and her famed circle at Münster. Father Lemcke expressed genuine surprise that he and Mitri were in the same diocese, and also felt sad to hear that the old priest's health was failing. As Father Lemcke was not happy with the trustees in Holy Trinity, and as Bishop Kenrick had found a German-speaking priest to take his place in the parish, the prelate sensed that Mitri and the German priest might be a good match together in the Allegheny parish.

On his way to Loretto, Father Lemcke was able to observe firsthand the grandeur and the ruggedness of Pennsylvania as well as the nature and character of its inhabitants. As was then the custom, Lemcke, as a German-speaker, sent word ahead to the local communities of his arrival so that they might be able to make confession and ask his advice on spiritual matters. One such group of Catholics, from Switzerland and Germany, welcomed Father Lemcke with open arms. It had been years since a priest had blessed them with a visit, especially one who could communicate in their native tongue.

After serving the Catholics of the community Father Lemcke went on to Loretto. He met Mitri as he neared the settlement, and he wrote of the introduction:

> As we had gone a couple of miles through the woods, I caught sight of a sled, drawn by a pair of vigorous horses and in the sled a half recumbent traveler, on every lineament of whose face could be read a character of distinction. He was outwardly dressed in a sort of threadbare overcoat; and on his head, a peasant's hat, so worn and dilapidated that no one could have received it from the garbage of the streets. It occurred to me that some accident had happened to the old gentleman; and that he was compelled to this singular mode of conveyance. . . . Tom, my guide, who was trotting ahead, turned around and pointed to the old man, said: "Here comes the priest." I immediately coaxed up my nag to the sled. "Are you really the pastor of Loretto?" said I [in German]. "I am, sir." "Prince Gallitzin?" "At your service, sir," he said with a laugh. "You are probably astonished" — he continued after I handed him a letter from the Bishop of Philadelphia

— at the strangeness of my equipage? But there is no help for it. You have no doubt already found out . . . you need not dream of a carriage-road. You could not drive ten yards without danger of an overturn. I am prevented, since a fall which I have had, from riding on horseback, and it would be impossible for me now to travel on foot. Beside, I carry along everything required for the celebration of the holy Mass. I am now going to a spot where I have a mission, and where the holy sacrifice has been announced for today. Go to Loretto and make yourself at home, until my return to night; unless, indeed, you should prefer to accompany me. You may be interested in the visit."

Mitri was headed for Joshua Parrish's clearing, and Father Lemcke followed him enthusiastically. There they found a cabin decorated as a temporary chapel and already filled with the local faithful, prayer books in hand, awaiting the arrival of their pastor. Father Gallitzin received their greetings and introduced Father Lemcke with the added pleasure of announcing his presence to hear confessions in German. Mitri took a chair in one corner of the main room of the cabin and heard confessions in English while Lemcke took a chair in another corner and heard confessions in his native tongue. Mass was then celebrated, followed by a group of baptisms, instructions, and then a joyous dinner that became a genuine feast of welcome.

Once at Loretto, Father Lemcke began the long process of familiarizing himself with the people and with the stunning setting of the Alleghenies. He found his host everything that he had heard, and the two had much to discuss concerning events in Europe, the intellectual and religious situation there, and the remarkable progress of Mitri in Loretto. This was a strong Catholic community, obvious in the many Catholics who greeted him, and in the abundant respect paid to the pastor. A general sense of amity pervaded the region as well, born of stolid faith and dedication.

A more intimate introduction to the Loretto congregation presented itself the following Sunday. High Mass was celebrated by Father Lemcke, and Mitri delivered a sermon in English, while music was provided by a small organ. The new assistant was surprised at Mitri's agility, moving as easily as he did during the Mass. Father Lemcke was also astonished when Gallitzin completed his sermon on pride and the virtue of humility in English and began anew in German. Mitri announced that, as there was now a priest who could deliver the sermon in better German than he, the matter would be left to Father Lemcke, who was then expected to deliver a complete sermon on the spot. Lemcke did his best, later asking his host about the extemporaneous sermon. Mitri answered simply: "A missionary must be ready at a moment's notice to produce the old and the new."

The very next day, Mitri took Father Lemcke to Ebensburg. Here the young priest watched as the pastor took what looked like a survey of each house. Mitri went from door to door, spoke with the inhabitants in English, and then made notes. At last, as night fell, Mitri led him to the home of the county treasurer, Mr. Ivory. Mrs. Ivory was particularly delighted to have Mitri as a guest; she had been raised by the priest in the small orphanage of the house at Loretto. After the evening meal, Mitri unfolded the paper he had used earlier. It was full of names with added comments and notes.

He told Father Lemcke: "Here are the Catholics who will support you. I will also pay you a hundred dollars a year if you come once a month to preach in German at Loretto. You have seen the log chapel in this town. You can lodge here at Mr. Ivory's. Mrs. Ivory is a good cook."

"Why not in Loretto?" asked Father Lemcke.

"You might be cold in my presbytery. Except for the kitchen, there is only one fireplace."

"But how can I live at Ebensburg and minister at Ebensburg when it is the one place where there are no Germans? You know I can't speak English."

"All the better to learn," Mitri announced firmly.

Uncertain, Father Lemcke returned to Philadelphia and gave a full report to Bishop Kenrick. He expressed his regret to Kenrick that Mitri had obviously been disappointed, suggesting as he had that Father Lemcke serve outside of Loretto. The bishop then produced a letter from Gallitzin full of praise for the young priest. The bishop suggested that Lemcke take the post, but he did offer another posting as well, in Pittsburgh. Traveling to the city of the three rivers, Father Lemcke was disappointed instantly by the absence of a strong sense of community,

The first meeting of Fr. Peter Lemcke and Fr. Gallitzin in 1834.

by the obsession of amassing wealth at the expense of the poor immigrants, and by the widely dispersed Catholics who struggled against the anti-Catholic sentiment of the Protestant majority. Such a place stood in sharp contrast with the thriving Catholic center of Loretto. As time passed, Father Lemcke stood more and more in awe of Mitri and of the full breadth of his achievements in the Alleghenies. By Christmas, Father Lemcke was in Ebensburg.

For the next six years, the young priest worked closely with Mitri, deepening both his regard and fondness for the prince priest whom he saw sincerely as a hero of the American Church. Thus, when he was able to establish a new parish to the north of Ebensburg and Loretto, Father Lemcke proposed to name it "Gallitzin." This was completely unacceptable to Mitri who had a different name in mind. He asked the new community to be christened Carrolltown in memory of Archbishop John Carroll.

As Mitri's friend, assistant, and confessor, Father Lemcke was present at the pastor's side at the end in 1840, succeeding him in the difficult position of pastor of Loretto. Calling Gallitzin "the noblest, purest, and most godly man I have ever met," Father Lemcke was not intimidated by the towering presence of his predecessor. Rather, he did all he could to preserve the memory of Mitri, even after leaving Loretto for other assignments. Twenty years after the death of Mitri, Father Lemcke authored a biography of the priest in German, *Leben und Wirken des Prinzen Demetrius Augustine Gallitzin,* published in Munster in 1861. Translated in 1940 by Reverend Joseph Plumpe (then a professor at the Pontifical College Josephinum in Ohio) and published under the title *The Life and Work of Prince Demetrius Gallitzin,* the biography presented a detailed and generally accurate account of Mitri's life. While he was not a trained historian and the anecdotal style often lacks dates, Father Lemcke did have a fine memory and used a large amount of primary source material. Prince Mitri was a superbly organized pastor, retaining all his correspondence and making copies of any important letters he might send. He also recorded his daily occurrences and kept records, in perfect order, of the parish happenings and events. The bulk of his letters and records were kept in a trunk which passed to Father Lemcke when he became pastor of Loretto and these documents were used extensively in the writing of the biography. The value of Father Lemcke's effort only increased in the years that followed as the collection was divided up and many letters and records were lost. Lemcke himself died on November 29, 1882.

Both of Mitri's biographers — Heyden and Lemcke — used a good part of their writings to preserve the record of Mitri's last years, offering a vivid picture of the commitment by the priest to give of himself even at the moment of death. The account is a painful one, for Mitri suffered terribly in his last years, though he bore his mounting ailments with patience and acceptance.

Aside from the loss of his teeth and the other minor medical complaints that were a part of life on the frontier and of his advancing years, Mitri entered 1834 in perfect health. That year, while on one of his pastoral missions, he was thrown from his black mare and injured his leg. The damage was aggravated by the symptoms of a hernia. Mitri's days of riding were ended, which was an exceptionally cruel blow to an expert equestrian who relied upon the horse to perform his daily duties.

To solve his transportation problem, Mitri adopted a sleigh. Intended for use in the winter, the sleigh was a practical way of journeying through the forest. As Father Lemcke noted, Mitri transported all of his necessary items for saying Mass while at the same time avoiding undue stress on his leg. A wild story soon circulated that Mitri, who never complained about the injury, was not seriously hurt and instead had adopted the sleigh as a symbolic gesture until all his debts were paid.

From 1834 to the summer of 1839, Mitri continued nearly at full energy as pastor. He paid off the last of his debts, wrote the *Six Letters of Advice to the Gentlemen Presbyterian Parsons*, and went about his daily pastorate as though he were still unmarked by failing health. This changed in 1839. As Father Lemcke wrote:

> When I first saw Gallitzin he was indeed very thin, and his appearance frail. But his carriage was erect, his walk firm and quick. His voice was loud and sonorous, his look keen and determined. However, toward the year 1839 all this changed very noticeably, and I was quite concerned. He began to walk stooped, and his step became uncertain. Occasionally during his sermons and other functions the flame of his old voice would fail him, and his sermons passed into soft weeping, though this proved a more impressive lesson than could have been conveyed by words; for the whole parish sat deeply moved and edified, and wept with him.

Word soon spread that Mitri was fading fast, and Father Heyden wrote a letter of sympathy. As ever, Mitri refused to allow his infirmities to become a topic of concern or conversation. He wrote back to Heyden:

> The account you had of my illness was not founded in fact. What may have given rise to it is that I was for one Sunday only, prevented from appearing at the holy altar by pains in the lower joints, which alarmed some of those who being in the habit of seeing me there every Sunday, concluded I must be very ill. In Chambersburg, they have me dead and buried.

Mitri's optimistic self-appraisal was not matched by the reality of his health. His hip and hernia were growing worse, so much so that the simple act of walking was painful. As a result, the pastoral missions, which necessitated the bumpy sleigh rides through the forests, were agonizing. The winter of 1839-1840 added to his suffering, for the freezing winter air, the snows, and the perilous journeys over mountains and hills made his normal sick calls and other priestly duties even harder for him to endure without complaint. With his joints cold and brittle, his body aching from the snow, and his lungs filled with numbing, chilly air, Mitri came out of the winter utterly exhausted. But his commitment to the parish did not waver, and he continued at his regular pace throughout Lent. Each service, each Mass, and each confession appeared to drain his energies.

As Easter approached, Mitri had a chance encounter with Dr. Aristide Rodrique, a young physician from Philadelphia who had settled in Ebensburg in 1834. The priest asked for the doctor's assessment and was told without hesitation that he should begin resting immediately. Bed rest, warmth, and a respite from his labors were necessary if he should have any hope of regaining his strength. Mitri thanked the physician warmly but then stated simply that such a prescription was impossible to take because of the Lenten needs of his flock. Perhaps after Easter he could take some rest. Mitri then returned to Loretto where he spent most of Holy Week sitting in the freezing confessionals of the local churches.

Finally, Easter Sunday arrived with Mitri still in the confessional.

The confessional screen and chair used by Gallitzin. (Photo courtesy of Mr. James Seiler.)

He heard the sins of his parishioners right to the start of the Mass at ten, but by then he was so grievously exhausted and sick that he could not celebrate the High Mass. During the Low Mass he delivered what a few in the congregation realized was his last sermon. The homily was all too brief, focusing on the Resurrection. He finished with his last exclamation of Christ on the Cross: "It is consummated."

With Easter's duties concluded, Mitri was finally willing to take some rest. By then, his health was so poor that he could not find the energy to get out of bed. Messengers went out of Loretto to inform the priests. Lemcke was unable to come at once because of an injury to his heel caused by an ax blow while cutting firewood. He sent a trusted parishioner to Loretto. That individual returned with the terrible news that Mitri was bedridden and quite ill. Father Bradley arrived, and wrote to Father Heyden that the Apostle of the Alleghenies was deathly ill.

Mitri was at first certain that he would recover, but as the days passed he realized that he was growing weaker. The week after Easter he began to agree with Dr. Rodrique that death was approaching, and calmly, in good cheer and much like his prince father before him, Mitri put his affairs in order. He was especially pleased that he had completed the payment of all his debts, leaving Loretto in the black. He also made a comprehensive will that was witnessed by three parishioners.

The principal heir to Mitri's holdings was the Bishop of Philadelphia, to whom he left the church, farm, chapel house, all lands (including a square of six lots in Loretto he had intended to use as a new church), and "all the appurtenances thereunto belonging." The residue of the estate was left in trust to his three executors. The five horses, three cows, two-horse wagons, two violins, seeds, furniture, and 574 books were to be divided to finance four primary projects and purposes. First, there was an amount for the relief of poor widows and orphans. Second, Masses were to be celebrated for the repose of the souls of the faithfully departed. Third, a new church was to be built. Money was also to be set aside for Suzannah Christy, Sarah Durbin, Ann Storm, and Francis and Hugh McConnell, who were raised from childhood by Mitri.

As it was essential to Father Lemcke to reach his bedside, Mitri sent his trusty sleigh to transport the hobbled priest. Father Lemcke arrived in time to meet with the doctors, who informed him that there was nothing to be done medically, save a procedure to relieve some of the pressure caused by the hernia which would ease Mitri's suffering. He agreed, telling his friend Father Lemcke:

> My will is made. I trust that so far as I am concerned, I can depart in peace and that no one will lose anything through me, but there may be ever something left over. Now I wish the last sacraments, and then do with me what you like.

Father Lemcke celebrated Mass at midnight in Mitri's room, along with the entire household. After the Mass, the doctors performed the operation which proved a success and eased the dying priest's agony. The following morning the people of Loretto gathered at the chapel house and began the day's procession past Mitri's bed. Tearfully, they came to bid him farewell. Even with his strength failing, he was still able to call each parishioner by name, bestow his blessing, and give one and all a warm smile. All remembered one particular man of the parish who refused to give up drink and was ever unrepentant but came to Mitri's bed to bid farewell. Gallitzin raised his hand, pointed a finger at the sinner, and shook his head gently with disapproval. The man fell to his knees and wept so uncontrollably that Gallitzin expressed regret that he had not left him money. He implored the other parishioners not to forget him in his needs.

On May 4, Father Lemcke was joined at Mitri's side by Father Heyden, and the two remained at prayer for the next two days. Loretto parishioners shared their prayers in the chapel and the church as the last hours came for Mitri. He had served the Alleghenies for four decades, always present, always dedicated. Entire generations of Americans had gazed upon him in his labors, knowing that he always managed to face life with faith and vigor.

Now America and the world would endure the wrenching agony of losing a man of God whose goodness shone as a light in the chaos of social and political change. The people of Loretto realized in their sorrow that Mitri had never truly been one of them. He had come to their aid as a being quite remarkable and unique. He was a nobleman, but that distinction had little to do with rank or titles. Mitri's nobility was of the soul, where faith glistened with clarity and grace. Mitri had focused on the day-to-day pilgrimages of simple settlers in a new land, understanding the destiny and promise of America as he recognized divine grace in the individual soul. To this end he had given his life, hour by hour, day by day, alone and uncomforted. He was a prince of the pastoral ministry, and now he was going to Christ, his Lord.

On May 6, 1840, in the early evening, Demetrius Gallitzin breathed his last. The doors to the room were opened to announce that Mitri was gone. The first wails of sorrow echoed across Loretto, to be echoed throughout the nation and the world. In Baltimore, Bishop Kenrick received the news while attending the provincial council. He rose and informed the council fathers that the Apostle of the Alleghenies and great apologist for the faith was dead. All were saddened by the news of America's loss.

Prince Demetrius Gallitzin lay in state in St. Mary's Chapel for four days and was viewed by crowds from all over Cambria County and beyond. Fathers Heyden, Lemcke, and Bradley presided over the obsequies, taking turns to lead the throngs of the faithful in the prayers for the dead. No formal public announcement was made of the death, for there was no need. The grief of the American people spread quickly on its own.

The original coffin containing the remains of Fr. Gallitzin in Loretto.

Photo courtesy of the Prince Gallitzin Chapel House

A Requiem Mass was celebrated by Father Heyden, who preached a homily in English, and he was joined by Father Lemcke who preached in German. Outside, an enormous crowd filled the streets of Loretto to watch the priests lead the funeral procession in the final rites. The grief of the people was palpable and vivid as they gazed upon the zinc coffin encased in a second layer of walnut. The coffin was fashioned by Louis Sturm for the sum of eight dollars.

The simple burial was in keeping with Mitri's earnest request. However, ten years later the coffin was disinterred and placed in a vault in front of the new church. A monument was erected on the site and adorned with an inscription composed by Bishop Kenrick:

SACRUM MEMORIAE
Dem. A. E. Principibus Gallitzin —
nat. XXII Decemb.
A.D. MDCCLXX.
Qui Schismate. ejurato, Ad. Sacer-
dotium evectus
Sacro Ministerio per. tot. hanc.
reb. perfunctus
Fide, zelo. Charitate. insignis.
Heic. obiit die
VI Maii, A.D. MDCCCXL

(Sacred to the memory of Dem. A. of the Gallitzin Prince — born Dec. 22, 1770, who, having renounced Schism, was raised to the Priesthood. Exercised the sacred ministry through the whole of this region. Distinguished for faith, zeal, and charity. Died May 6, 1840.)

In 1970, a bicentennial celebration of the birth of Mitri was held by the diocese of Altoona-Johnstown under the leadership of Bishop John Hogan. The celebration climaxed on May 31, 1970, when a concelebrated Mass was held at the Loretto shrine grounds. The principal concelebrant was John Cardinal Krol, then Archbishop of Philadelphia, and other concelebrants were Archbishop Luigi Raimondi, Apostolic Delegate to the United States; Bishop Hogan; Bishop George Leech of Harrisburg; Bishop Vincent Leonard of Pittsburg; Bishop William Connare of Greensburg; and Bishop Urban McGarry, T.O.R., of Bhagalpur, India. The sermon was delivered by Lawrence Cardinal

Shehan, Archbishop of Baltimore and a distant successor to Archbishop Carroll who ordained Mitri in 1795. The cardinal's words that speak of Demetrius Gallitzin for any age and any setting:

> O happy Prince, who gave up parents and friends and rank and all earthly possessions to serve the Prince of Peace and King of Kings! O Happy priest, who from the day of ordination to the day of death spent a life completely dedicated to priestly pastoral work and the love of the great High Priest! O happy you, Bishop, priests and people of the diocese who have inherited from the founder of your local Church and have faithfully preserved such a tradition of faith and loyalty and Christian love!

The current tomb of Fr. Gallitzin, c. 1818.

Appendix

The History of Loretto After Reverend Gallitzin

The death of Reverend Demetrius Gallitzin brought an end to a forty-year era during which Loretto was born, fostered, and prospered through the work and prayer virtually of one man. Spiritual care of the many souls of Loretto now passed to Reverend Peter Lemcke, who spent four years preserving Mitri's legacy. During this time, the 1840s, the growing population of Catholics and churches in Pennsylvania made another see for the state necessary. Pope Gregory XVI decreed on August 8, 1843, the new see of Pittsburgh; Michael O'Connor became its first bishop, and Loretto was placed — with western Pennsylvania — under his jurisdiction.

Three years later a Franciscan friar, Brother Giles Carroll, arrived in Pittsburgh from Ireland with a plea for help. The Irish potato famine, which was devastating Ireland, had brought the Franciscan community in that country to near starvation, making it impossible for the friars to educate the young. Friar Carroll hoped to migrate with his fellow Franciscans to the Pittsburgh diocese, and Bishop O'Connor immediately wrote to the archbishop of Tuam, the superior of the Franciscans in Ireland, to offer a formal invitation to the Franciscans to settle in his diocese.

Later that year, Brother Carroll and six Franciscans came to Pittsburgh and began looking for suitable sites to establish themselves. After visiting several locations, the friars settled on what they felt was an ideal location: Loretto. Father Gallitzin had set aside a large tract of land to be at the disposal of the pastor of St. Michael's, and the successor to Lemcke, Reverend Hugh Gallagher (1844-1852), leased several acres with the understanding that they would be a monastery and school.

The terms of the lease were clear: the Franciscans were to pay five dollars annual rent to the pastor of St. Michael's, and the pastor was to enjoy the privilege of chopping firewood from the property.

The Franciscans cut trees, gathered tools and supplies, and the first building was completed within a year. The new school was nearly finished in three years, and Bishop O'Connor journeyed from Pittsburgh to celebrate the first Mass in the new chapel of what was the future St. Francis Academy on August 2, 1850. In 1858, the academy was granted a charter permitting it to bestow academic certificates. From this foundation grew St. Francis Seminary and also St. Francis College, which has been a fixture in education in western Pennsylvania.

The arrival of the Franciscans in Loretto in 1847 was followed within a year by the members of the congregation of the Sisters of Mercy. They, too, settled on part of the tract set aside by Reverend Gallitzin, creating a monastery, convent, and a school — the Mount Aloysius Academy for girls. The academy was inaugurated in the Autumn of 1853 and remained at Loretto until 1896, when the sisters moved to Cresson. The present site where the academy once stood is now near the shrine of Our Lady of the Alleghenies, one of the stations visited by pilgrims taking the Loretto Pilgrimage.

The dedication of the statue was held on October 10, 1899, by Archbishop John Ireland, archbishop of St. Paul and one of the most respected leaders of the American Church. Also in attendance were the Apostolic Delegate, Archbishop (later Cardinal) Sebastiano Martinelli, O.S.A., the governor of Pennsylvania, numerous other dignitaries, and a congregation of some 5,000.

Even as these spiritual benefactions were coming to fruition, in 1852 Reverend Gallagher started work on the third church at Loretto, the first to be built of brick. Sadly, Reverend Gallagher did not see its completion. In 1852, he headed west to California and was replaced as pastor by his brother, Reverend Joseph Gallagher. The church was dedicated on January 6, 1854, by the bishop of Philadelphia, St. John Neumann, who had been appointed bishop in 1852. One of the spiritual models for the Church in the United States, St. John Neumann was beatified in 1963 and canonized in 1977 by Pope Paul VI. The new church was named initially St. Mary's; however, Father Gallagher changed the title in 1870 to St. Michael the Archangel, in honor of the earlier churches built by the prince.

Twenty-one years after Father Gallagher embraced the earlier name for the Loretto church, the remains of Mitri were exhumed and placed in a new coffin, with a metal, airtight casket. Over the crypt was placed a bronze statue that commemorated the priest and served as merely a foretaste of the much larger church that was to come.

The Catholic industrialist and president of Carnegie Steel, Charles M. Schwab, decided to celebrate the hundredth anniversary of Father Gallitzin's first Mass in the new church at Loretto by making a gift of a brand new church. Schwab graduated from St. Francis College in 1880, and soon after began working for United States Steel. Rising rapidly, he became president of the company, but he never forgot Loretto, where he had spent most of his youth. He thus informed the pastor of Loretto, Reverend Ferdinand Kittell (pastor from 1891-1927), of his desire to build a sizable church for the new century. The gift was more than timely, for the brick church was in need of extensive renovations and expansion; the congregation was growing ever larger, but so too were the number of pilgrims coming to visit the tomb of Mitri.

Donating the whole of the $150,000 needed for construction, the Schwabs made possible the razing of the old church and the start of construction on January 10, 1900. The consecration of the new church took place on October 2, 1901; the walls were anointed in twelve places with holy chrism (denoted today by twelve crosses).

Named the Church of St. Michael the Archangel, the fourth and most elaborate of the churches at Loretto is of a Romanesque style of architecture, with various features done in the Gothic style, combining traditionally rounded Romanesque arches, especially in the thirty-two-foot tower of Ohio Cut Sandstone, with Gothic arches and flying buttresses. The roof was made of Akron red tiles, and the three bells were donated in honor of Father Kittell, Mr. and Mrs. Charles Schwab, and Mr. and Mrs. John Schwab. Typical of the Romanesque, the church was built in the shape of a Latin cross.

The church interior included four altars of Carrara marble of a Gothic design, stained-glass windows, a communion rail of Mexican onyx, pews of quartered red oak, and an organ. The altars were imported from Italy, with statues of Mary and Joseph that were gifts from Mrs. Charles Schwab and Mrs. Pauline Schwab respectively. The stained-glass windows depicted scenes of the Annunciation, the Visitation, the Child Jesus in the Temple, the Holy Family, and Christ appearing to St. Mary Magdalene.

The Church of St. Michael's c. 1901, shortly after completion.

Contrary to popular belief, the windows are not Tiffany. The organ was the only element of the church not paid for by the Schwab family. That $8,000 instrument was funded by Andrew Carnegie. Long a stop on the Loretto Pilgrimage, St. Michael's was declared a minor basilica by Pope John Paul II on September 9, 1996.

A few months before the consecration of the new church, an announcement was sent to the Church in the United States. Pope Leo XIII, on June 1, 1901, decreed that a new diocese was created for western Pennsylvania between the dioceses of Pittsburgh and Harrisburg. The hope of Mitri that his region should have its own bishop at last came to pass. However, Loretto was not the episcopal see, for the Holy See had designated the important city of Altoona. The vicar-general of the diocese of Scranton, Right Reverend Monsignor Eugene A. Garvey was named the first bishop of Altoona. He took as a major focus of his tenure to develop further Catholic education. In September, 1912, the Loretto seminary was designated by Bishop Garvey to be the diocesan seminary, with theology students attending St. Francis College to complete their academic studies. The college also received permission in 1920 to grant academic degrees, a major step in establishing the school as an education leader in western Pennsylvania.

In 1926, the gathering of religious communities in the Altoona diocese increased when Bishop John McCort, second bishop of Altoona, issued an invitation to a community of French Carmelite nuns to migrate to the United States. As it was, his letter could not have come at a better time for the nuns — in a similar position to the Irish Franciscans decades before — were facing the death of the community from the irreparable damage done to their house and its environs during the terrible fighting of World War I. The nuns prayed for the assistance of St. Thérèse of Lisieux, and only a short time after the start of their novena the letter from Bishop McCort reached their convent.

The Carmelite nuns reached New York in October, 1926. Once in Altoona, they took up temporary residence with the Sisters of Mercy in Cresson until their cloistered convent could be finished. Their proposed house was constructed on land offered to them by the Franciscans at Loretto. The site was opposite a picturesque hill on which stood the summer residence of Charles Schwab. The industrialist heard of the sisters' need, and as providence would have it, his sister was a member of the Carmelite nuns. She had joined the Sisters of Charity at Greensburg and taken the name Sister Cecilia, but eventually she embraced the contemplative life of the Carmelite Order. Charles Schwab once again made a generous donation and guaranteed the completion of the convent in May, 1930. The finished house emulates the famed Carmel of Lisieux, France — the convent of St. Thérèse of Lisieux — and became another fixture on the Loretto Pilgrimage.

Ten years after the completion of the Carmelite convent, the diocese of Altoona celebrated the centenary of Mitri's death. At the encouragement of the pastor of Loretto, James Sass, P.R., Bishop Guilfoyle presided over the commemoration, including the celebration of a Pontifical Mass and a pageant on May 30, 1940.

Afterword

In 1999, the Diocese of Altoona-Johnstown celebrated the bicentennial of Father Gallitzin's arrival at McGuire's Settlement. Among the bicentennial events were a diocesan Mass, a pilgrimage to Loretto, a parish observance and Mass, and a commemoration of Mitri's first Christmas Mass on the mountain.

The events served as a moving recognition of the princely pastor's spiritual legacy. When he arrived in the Clearfields in 1799, Father Gallitzin found only a few hundred devout souls in the area. Two centuries later, there were more than 115,000 Catholics in the diocese of Altoona-Johnstown, served by 112 parishes. Where once Demetrius Gallitzin was the only priest in the area of the Alleghenies, 200 years later there are 121 active diocesan priests. In praising the spiritual legacy of Father Gallitzin, Bishop Joseph Adamec of Altoona-Johnstown declared in his homily at the Mass in the princely priest's honor on June 6, 1999:

> While the world was in turmoil, while political leaders jostled for positions, and while people worried about those things which would eventually end, Father Gallitzin devoted his time and energies to bring about a community that would reflect eternal values and be a foretaste of life to come.
>
> The Lord feeds us for that journey through both his Eucharist and his Word. Throughout time, He chooses those through whom we are to receive them. For two hundred years, due to the extreme generosity of self and deep dedication to the Church on the part of our evangelizer the Reverend Prince Demetrius A. Gallitzin, we of these Allegheny Mountains have been nourished by both. He came so that we might know

Fr. Demetrius Gallitzin, at about age 50, c. 1820

Christ and, knowing Christ, that we might reflect his very life to the world around us.

Our prayer can be that attributed to Pope John Paul II. It is a prayer composed for the occasion of a Eucharistic Procession. "Lord Jesus, from your altar illuminate this city with light and grace, so that it may reject the seduction of a materialistic concept of life, and defeat the selfishness that threatens it, the injustices that unsettle it, and the divisions with which it is afflicted."

The mission on which Father Gallitzin came continues, and the Church he came to nurture is continually coming into being. His vision ought to be ours. That vision is simply to be the Church that is called for in our time, an assembly of believers who faithfully and authentically witness to Christ — even 200 years later.